Praise for *Expect the Unexpected*

"This book captures the wonder of communication with the afterlife, a wonder felt not just by the deceased's families and friends, but also by the mediums themselves. Bill Philipps's insiders' accounts, written with energy and conviction, demonstrate again and again the maxim of professional mediumship: the dead are always right."
— JULIA ASSANTE, PhD, author of *The Last Frontier*

"*Expect the Unexpected* is a down-to-earth, honest account of how spirits communicate with Bill Philipps, how he embraced his gift, and how you can learn to recognize the signs our spirit loved ones use to guide us in our lives. . . . His sincerity, devotion to the process, and enthusiasm in spreading knowledge make him a genuine teacher."
— from the foreword by MAUREEN HANCOCK, author of *The Medium Next Door*

"This book not only gives evidence of life after death but also gives a very accurate view of the struggles a pure psychic medium goes through. Bill Philipps is real, down-to-earth, humble, and obviously very gifted, and I'm so grateful he wrote this book. Another hundred pages would still be too short."
— ECHO BODINE, author of *Echoes of the Soul* and *The Gift*

"[Bill] Philipps writes with humility, respect, and compassion. It's clear that his intent is to help, not to impress. He speaks, not from a pedestal, but toe-to-toe with the people who seek his help. Whether or not your customers are convinced about spirit contact, they will find this book to be a lighthouse on the path to healing and serenity."
— ANNA JEDRZIEWSKI, *Retailing Insight*

Expect the Unexpected

Expect the Unexpected

Bringing Peace, Healing, and Hope
from the Other Side

BILL PHILIPPS

with William Croyle

Foreword by Maureen Hancock

New World Library
Novato, California

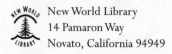

New World Library
14 Pamaron Way
Novato, California 94949

Text design by Tona Pearce Myers

Library of Congress Cataloging-in-Publication Data
Philipps, Bill, date.
Expect the unexpected : bringing peace, healing, and hope from the other side / Bill Philipps, psychic medium, with William Croyle.
    pages   cm
ISBN 978-1-60868-367-3 (hardcover : alk. paper) — ISBN 978-1-60868-368-0 (ebook)
1. Philipps, Bill, date. 2. Mediums—United States—Biography. 3. Psychics —United States—Biography. I. Title.
BF1283.P485A3 2015
133.9'1092—dc23   2015020080

First paperback printing, June 2017
ISBN 978-1-60868-495-3
Ebook ISBN 978-1-60868-496-0
Printed in Canada on 100% postconsumer-waste recycled paper

New World Library is proud to be a Gold Certified Environmentally Responsible Publisher. Publisher certification awarded by Green Press Initiative. www.greenpressinitiative.org

10   9   8   7   6   5   4   3   2   1

To my mother, Yvonne,
who taught me that our light
can never be extinguished

CONTENTS

FOREWORD

Bill Philipps is both a psychic medium and spiritual teacher. He realized in his younger years — as I had realized about myself — that he was different and possessed an uncanny ability to see, feel, and hear spirits. Having experienced a heart-wrenching and harrowing path through childhood, Bill shares his journey from the depths of darkness to healing, and to understanding and embracing his gift. After the physical passing of his mother three weeks before his fifteenth birthday, he experienced a profound spirit connection with her. The memory of seeing his mother whole again, no longer tormented by the darkness of addiction, eventually sparked Bill's need to share his compelling story.

There has been an evident shift in belief systems around the globe. Millions are reaching out to find answers, to understand death in the face of tragedy and loss. According to the Reverend Andrew M. Greeley, a sociologist at the University of Chicago, 81 percent of Americans believe in an afterlife. This helps explain the growing spiritual interest of Americans demonstrated by the success of television shows, live mediumship events, and books on the subject.

Expect the Unexpected is a down-to-earth, honest account of how spirits communicate with Bill Philipps, how he nurtured his gift, and how you can learn to recognize the signs our spirit loved ones use to guide us in our lives.

Bill goes beyond the facile anecdote and shares some of the most chilling and soul-shaking experiences unearthed by his work. Through many testimonials, his clients share their heartfelt connections, helping us to know that love is stronger than death, and spirit communication is possible for all. He squelches the fear associated with death and provides his audiences and readers with healing and an accessible understanding of death, dying, and the inspiring connections beyond the grave.

When I first met Bill, I was immediately drawn to his passion for his work and to his message. Only a handful of mediums come from a place of no ego — and Bill is one of those rare gems. You know how it feels when you meet someone and instantly feel connected, and you resonate on the same level? That's what transpired in our first meeting. His goal is the same as mine: to spread knowledge, healing, and love to all.

This book is the story of Bill's personal journey, but it is a story that instructs us all. His sincerity, devotion to the process, and enthusiasm in spreading knowledge make him a genuine teacher. May Bill, with his messages, teachings, and abilities, flourish as he helps legions of people heal after loss. People need to know not only that their loved ones continue to exist in some form and dimension but also that their loved ones still play a role in their lives here on earth.

— Maureen Hancock, author of *The Medium Next Door*

Introduction

PEACE, HEALING, and HOPE

P̀sychic medium.

The term conjures images of a flashing neon sign suspended in a dark window of a rundown storefront on a desolate urban street. Inside is a shadowy room flush with metaphysical decor and the faint sound of New Age music. An ornately dressed woman with a deceiving smile sits behind a shiny deck of tarot cards, maybe even a crystal ball. She is anxiously waiting to spew vague claims and suck money from the vulnerable, who are seeking nothing more than a glint of hope to heal their pain or enhance their lives.

At least that's how I envisioned one — until I discovered that I was one myself. As a six-foot-five-inch, thirty-one-year-old suburban businessman from Southern California with an operatic voice and a degree from the San Francisco Conservatory of Music, I'm pretty confident that I shatter the stereotype. In fact, my entire life story defies belief.

I was the product of alcoholic and drug-addicted parents, witnessing filth as a child to which no one of any age should be

1

subjected. I was kidnapped by my mom when I was six years old, hustled across the country from the West Coast to the East Coast, where I was homeless for most of the next three years. I was nine when I was shipped back to my dad because my mom couldn't sober up enough to take care of me. And I was fourteen when I returned to New York to hold my mom's hand and watch her die.

That was my childhood in a nutshell. Depressing? Absolutely. In fact, it was often a living nightmare. But everything happens for a reason, and it was that tumultuous chain of events that led to my extraordinary life today.

Two days after my mom's death, she visibly appeared to me from "the other side" to let me know that she was spiritually alive, and that the afterlife was a wonderful place to be. A few weeks after her funeral, a strip-mall psychic in California, who had no idea who I was or what I had just experienced with my mom three thousand miles away, literally pulled me off the street to tell me I had an "amazing gift."

I was an ordinary teenager just hanging out at the mall with my friends. I dismissed her as some kind of whack job.

But three years later, there was no denying it. The spirits were there, dwelling in my head all day and every day, desperately trying to communicate with their living loved ones through me. Picture a mob of people — friendly, but persistent — perpetually knocking on every door and window of your home. That's what my mind endured from the spirits. I tried hard to ignore them, refuting their presence, but their energy was too strong. I couldn't shake them.

I reluctantly conducted readings for friends, hoping to satisfy the spirits so they would leave me alone and infiltrate someone else's psyche, but that strategy backfired. Word on the other side evidently spread, because my mind was getting inundated with restless spirits every day.

My popularity was also expanding among those on this side. People found out that I wasn't just conducting readings, that I was also doing them with compelling accuracy, revealing specific personal details that nobody could have known without someone close to them — someone who had died — telling me. This phenomenon was incredible even to me, the messenger. I was somehow able to connect those on earth with the deceased. Or, to state it more specifically, I was acknowledging the spirits of the dead who were determined to use me as a channel to relay messages to their living loved ones.

But how was this happening? And why was it happening to me?

With testimonies from a wide spectrum of people — of various races, backgrounds, and occupations, and even from onetime skeptics whose attitudes were initially nothing short of cynical — *Expect the Unexpected* is a firsthand account of how spirits communicate with me. In it I explain why I believe they chose me to do this, how I work with them to ultimately convey their messages to you, how you can receive signs from them without the help of a medium, and how you can use those signs to improve your daily life. The testimonies that appear between chapters are from some of my thousands of past and current clients, who so graciously agreed to share their profound experiences to help you understand how the spirits work. The quotes at the beginnings of the chapters are words of inspiration written by me but inspired by the spirits during my meditations.

There are those who will not want anything to do with this gift I have (you can count my own grandmother in that category). But that's okay. I'm not out to convert nonbelievers into believers or to disrupt someone's faith, as Grandma will attest. I do not force people to take an interest in what I do. Unless you are open to knowing that a spirit is trying to communicate with you, I will not tell you; it is a rule of mine by which the spirits must abide. But an inordinate number of people around the world do believe, or are at least curious enough to give the spirits a chance.

While I don't have all the answers to the mysteries of this life or the next, I am confident this book will give you three elements of comfort that we all want in our daily lives. These are elements that I attempt to bring to all those who seek my help in connecting them with the other side: peace, healing, and hope.

PART I

Discovering the Gift

Chapter 1

THE FIRST TIME

The universe works in mysterious ways to bring you exactly what you need at exactly the right time. Trust in your higher source.

I was fourteen years old when I had my first encounter with the spirit world. It was the starry summer evening of August 16, 1999. I'd been sound asleep in the upstairs guest room of an old home in Amityville, New York, on Long Island's south shore. The home, coincidentally, was two doors down from the one that sparked the popular 1970s book and movie *The Amityville Horror.*

Fortunately for me, there was nothing horrific about my encounter. In fact, it was quite the opposite. I was awakened by a warm, inviting glow near the ceiling in the far corner of the room. I sat up and rubbed my eyes to adjust to the radiance. And there she was.

A dazzling, young, gorgeous woman with deep-set eyes who was as fixated on me as I was on her. I was mesmerized by her majestic appearance as she gently hovered within the vibrant light, like an apparition. I sensed that she wanted to speak, but that she was waiting for me to make the first move. What did she want me to say? We both remained silent and patient, continuing our friendly stare-down for several seconds.

Finally, I blinked.

My body trembled when I realized who she was. It was an epiphany that blasted shockwaves to my core.

"Mom?" I said timidly, confounded by her presence.

She smiled.

The last time I had seen her was in the hospital two days earlier — when she died.

The first question I am usually asked when I begin to tell this story is: "How do you know it was not a dream?" I can assure you that while I've had some pretty vivid dreams in my life, this was absolutely not one of them. Trust me, I tried hard to convince myself that I wasn't seeing what I thought I was seeing. A ghost? A spirit? My dead mother? No way. But she was there. I was as awake as you are at this very moment.

Before I tell you what happened next, and to help you better understand the long-term significance of that unparalleled moment, I need to take you on a brief journey through my sordid childhood.

My mom and I shared a strong, unconditional, unbreakable mother-son bond, but our relationship during our short time together was toxic. That toxicity derived primarily from her heavy addiction to drugs and alcohol. She shared the drug habit with my dad, who also abused her. There was a vicious cycle of hate, anger, and degradation around me that I could not escape. That I turned out as normal as I did, considering the hell I was dragged through and witnessed as a child, is nothing short of a miracle. Sometimes I wonder how I made it out of my early years alive.

My mom boldly kidnapped me from my dad when I was six years old. The three of us had been living together at the time in Southern California with my paternal grandmother. My parents had been separated for a few months before that and then had reunited. Dad thought they had reconciled, but it was a devious ploy by my mom to gain his trust before running away with me. She had a boyfriend at the time and had formulated a plan to skip town with both of us. She implemented it one ordinary weekday morning after Dad left for work. She gave him a kiss, closed the front door behind him, then peered through the peephole to ensure that he was gone. As soon as he pulled away, she dashed to the bedroom and grabbed the bags she'd secretly packed the night before. She clutched my hand and told me to stay close to her as we scurried to a waiting car driven by our neighbor. The neighbor peeled out of the driveway and took us to the home of my mom's friend, who was expecting us. It was a well-orchestrated abduction by my mom, who had several helpful hands involved in her scheme.

When Dad came home later that day and realized we had vanished, he hit the streets to search for me. While we hid in my mom's friend's house, Dad telephoned in a rage, demanding to know if we were there. Afraid that he was about to find us, Mom rushed us out of the house. We fled down the street, desperately knocking on neighbors' doors until we were taken in by total strangers, a kindhearted family that I will never forget. Huddled inside, we could hear my dad calling me from the street: "Billlllllyyyyyy! Billlllllyyyyyy!" I was confused about how I was supposed to feel. In one sense, I felt safe with Mom. In another sense, it didn't feel right that Mom was hiding me from Dad. I could hear the desperation in his voice with each cry of my name.

With Mom fearing he might find us, we covertly left the strangers' home on foot after dark, about ten o'clock, for an abandoned school bus in a nearby ditch. Yes, a school bus in a ditch. Welcome to the drug underworld.

There I was, an innocent six-year-old boy up way past his bedtime, hiding out in a musty, broken-down bus lit with gas lanterns. While my friends were in their homes, blissfully and soundly sleeping in the comfort of their own beds, I was sur-rounded by eight adults smoking their crack pipes, jabbing themselves with needles, and performing sex acts on each other. I tried not to look as I maneuvered past them toward the back of the bus. I snuggled into the last seat, covered my ears, and closed my eyes in an attempt to escape the repulsiveness. My mom gave me a kiss on the forehead and told me she loved me before going to join her friends.

I don't know why, but strangely enough I felt relaxed and comforted within seconds, as if a force field of love were pro-tecting me. Everybody ignored me, and I was able, for the most part, to avoid watching and listening to their repugnant acts. Who knows, maybe *that* was actually my first encounter with the spirit world. Maybe that force field of love was the work of those on the other side shielding me from the evil that abounded. That bus was a horrific place to be, but somehow I safely made it through the night.

The next morning my mom, her boyfriend, and I boarded another bus — a working Greyhound this time — for a cross-country trip to Brooklyn, where her boyfriend had family. It was a wearisome three-thousand-mile trek over several days to a place that was not much different from the one I'd left. The phrase "It takes a village to raise a child" definitely applied to me, but the villagers raising me in New York left a lot to be desired.

Sometimes Mom and I lived in a crowded two-bedroom brownstone house with ten of her boyfriend's relatives. Other times we crashed at her boyfriend's sister's house, or with friends of theirs. I never felt wanted by our hosts; their homes were simply places to lay our heads, the atmospheres desolate. I was nothing more than another body in an already crowded place. We moved from house to house, apartment to apartment, even church to church. I never considered myself homeless, because there was always a roof above me; but by the federal government's definition, my situation was the essence of homeless.

I transferred to new schools multiple times each year, never settling into a routine or able to make many friends. My grades were decent, considering how many times I had to start over, but my real-world education outside of school overshadowed my academics. Drugs and violence were prevalent wherever we squatted. I was in the living room of a home one day with a couple of guys I barely knew — Mom was out on one of her drug binges — when one of the guys pulled a gun on the other during an argument. It scared me but didn't surprise me.

Some nights I went to bed and got a kiss goodnight from Mom. Most nights I tucked myself in and cried myself to sleep because she didn't come home. I never considered running away, but if I had I'm not sure anybody would have noticed I was gone. It was not unusual for Mom to disappear for weeks at a time as she wandered the streets looking for her drug fix. One Christmas Eve, I went to sleep wondering if she would make it home before Santa Claus arrived. She did . . . after police found her slumped on a cold metal bench in a train station. She was higher than Rudolph could fly. Merry Christmas.

My mom was a lost soul. As a result, so was I.

My turbulent life in New York lasted for three long years and ended, fittingly, when my mom went on another of her extended drug runs. We had been living temporarily with her boyfriend's sister, who decided enough was enough. I don't think she had anything against me; she simply decided she wasn't going to be responsible for raising her brother's girlfriend's son anymore. Who could blame her? I wasn't her kid. Technically I wasn't even family. She somehow found a way to reach my paternal grandmother in California. I hadn't seen anyone on that side of the family since the abduction.

"I'm not taking care of this boy anymore," she said to my grandma. "If you buy his plane ticket, he's all yours. I'll drive him to the airport."

Grandma and some other family members chipped in to buy the ticket. They actually had me fly from New York to Las Vegas, where my dad was temporarily working on a construction job. It sustained my new nomadic life. He and I lived there in an apartment for six months before we returned to Southern California, where it was New York all over again, but with palm trees. We lived in various hotels or moved from trailer to trailer and from school to school. When Dad wasn't working, he was lighting up his crack pipe. The constant moving lasted for about three years, until I was twelve, when I found refuge with my grandma. But Dad moved in with us a year later, still recklessly addicted.

During the years that I was away from my mom, I kept in close contact with her. I never got to see her, since there was no way my dad's family was going to take that chance, but I spoke with her by phone almost daily, or at least on days she was lucid enough to pick up a phone and talk. I cannot imagine how emotionally difficult it was for her when she sobered up and returned home to find that I had been sent back to my dad; I'm sure she immediately hit the streets again to try to escape the pain. It wasn't easy for me, either. Despite all that she put me through, she was still my mom. I knew she loved me, and I loved her. She just could not kick her habit. Somehow, even at a young age, I got that. But it was little consolation. She wanted what was best for me, as long as her needs were addressed first.

Flash forward to August of 1999 and the week leading to Mom's death.

It had been almost six years since I had seen her. I was a few weeks shy of my fifteenth birthday, and we still regularly talked by phone. She called me on Monday, August 9, to tell me she hadn't been feeling well for a while and was going to the hospital to have some tests done.

"You don't need to worry about it, Billy," she said. "Everything will be fine."

Two days later, on Wednesday, she called and told me she had a benign tumor on her pancreas. I don't know if she knew the truth and was trying to spare my feelings, or if it was just too difficult for her to come to terms with the real diagnosis, but at that time I had a strong suspicion that something was seriously wrong. She wasn't her usual bubbly self. She sounded as if the life had been sucked out of her. The clincher was when she ended the conversation very conclusively.

"I love you," she said, her voice cracking. "Good-bye, Billy."

I went to bed that night very sad. I knew she wasn't telling me everything, so the next day I called her boyfriend to find out what was really going on. Unfortunately, my intuition was correct.

"Billy, she has pancreatic cancer," he said, fighting through tears. "You need to get here. She is not doing well."

The phrase *pancreatic cancer* has long been synonymous with a quick death. I don't think I knew that at fourteen, but I could sense from the urgency in her boyfriend's voice that this could be the end of her life. Deeply distraught at the thought of losing my mom, I told my dad what was happening and pleaded with him to let me go see her. Of course, given their history and the con job she did on him when she kidnapped me, he did not believe for a second that she was sick. He released a long, loud, rambling rant about everything he hated about her and gave me multiple reasons why I wasn't going. But after stating his piece — and realizing by the look on my face just how much this meant to me, and remembering that I was almost fifteen and not six — he gave in and let me make my own decision. I took a red-eye flight on Friday and arrived in New York on Saturday morning.

I got to the hospital about 11 AM and was stunned by Mom's appearance, given that we had talked on the phone just three days earlier. She was hooked up to every tube and machine imaginable, including a breathing tube. Her eyes were closed, occasionally fluttering. She looked frail and lifeless. She was forty-one years old but looked twenty years older, if not thirty. I sat quietly in a chair at a little bit of a distance, just watching her, letting her sleep. I wondered if she would feel my presence and wake up on her own. When she didn't after a while, I tentatively walked to the side of her bed and touched my hand to hers. "Mom?" I softly whispered. "Mom?"

That's when all hell broke loose. At the sound of my voice, her eyes shot wide open. The breathing tube muffled her frantic screams. Her arms flailed as she yanked every tube and wire she could reach, ferociously ripping them off her body in an effort to stand up and wrap her arms around me for the first time in six years. Alarms triggered on every machine. Several nurses flew into the room to try to calm her down, resulting in a mini-brawl on the bed. One nurse swiftly escorted me out while the others teamed up to restrain Mom, literally tying her to the bed. She fought them with every ounce of what little energy she had, but lost.

I knew she would be shocked to see me, but I never expected that.

I wistfully left the hospital and went back to her boyfriend's house, the one in Amityville, to get some sleep. I returned to the hospital later that day, probably about 7 PM, and was accompanied to the room by a nurse just in case Mom went crazy again when she saw me. She was still in restraints, but unconscious. I talked to her but this time received no response. She looked peaceful, almost too peaceful. I could sense that the end was near. I told her I loved her, but that was it. I was a kid about to lose his mom. I really didn't know what more to say.

A little more than three hours later, at roughly 10:30 PM on August 14, I was at her bedside holding her hand as she quietly passed away.

I cried hard, as any child would at the loss of a parent. My life with Mom flashed before my eyes, and a flash was about all it took. We had such a short, difficult life together. Even when I was with her, she was rarely mentally with me. Essentially, I raised myself, and she filled in the gaps when she was able. I felt empty inside. I had few memories of her... few good ones, anyway. It was not the way a son and mother should part, but she was gone. It was over. There was nothing I could do. I had no idea, though, that there was something *she* could do.

When she appeared to me in the bedroom on August 16, she barely resembled the woman I had watched die two days earlier. In fact, she hardly looked like the mom I had known for nearly fifteen years — the old, ragged, tired woman who rolled the dice on the streets with her life each day. Within that brilliant light that night, she was much younger, healthier, and happier. Her complexion was immaculate. In a word, she was angelic. Ironically, I had never seen her look so alive.

After I had acknowledged that I knew who she was, she smiled and finally spoke to me. Her voice was soothing but had a persuasive tone. She said just two sentences, the first of which calmed my nerves considerably.

"Billy," she said, "I want you to know that I'm okay."

I smiled. If we could ask one question of our deceased loves ones, wouldn't it be: "Are you okay?" That's what we care about the most — for their sake now and for ours after this life. Even though Mom had succumbed to numerous temptations and had not lived a model life here on earth, she was in a better place. And her reassurance gave me profound comfort and a glimpse into the unknown that few people have ever experienced after losing someone close to them.

But she also gave me one more statement to ponder, one that was more ambiguous. "Also know that I will take care of you," she said.

Take care of me? I thought to myself. *Like my guardian angel?* I didn't know what that meant. Was it just a general statement about my life? Or was she referring to a specific situation? But before I could ask, she was gone. I cannot describe her transition from being there to not being there, because it was that quick. If I blinked, she vanished in that nanosecond. I would guess the entire encounter, from when I first saw her until she left, lasted thirty seconds, if that.

After she disappeared, the room returned to darkness and I was left alone to contemplate what had just happened. I stayed awake, trying to make sense of it, even talking to her with the hope that she might return, but she never did. I was happy that she had come to me and that she was obviously at peace, but sad that she was no longer physically present. Keep in mind that I was just fourteen years old and two days removed from her death after not seeing her for six years. I had barely started mourning her loss, and now she appears in some mystical form? I was confused. One thing I did know for sure was that I was not going to tell anybody what I had witnessed. Who would believe it? Everybody would think I had been hallucinating or dreaming.

About an hour later I fell asleep again. When I woke up with the morning sunlight streaming through the open window, I got out of bed and cautiously approached the corner in which Mom had appeared. I slowly ran my fingers along the walls and the floor. I gazed at the ceiling. I gracefully waved my hand through the air space she had occupied. I don't know exactly what I was searching for. Maybe she left something behind — tangible or intangible, an object or an energy — that I could share with somebody to prove she had been there.

That moment took me back to when I was maybe five or six years old. I would go to bed at night and sometimes see eyes or faces around me. It scared me so much that I begged Mom for a nightlight in my room. She obliged, but told me that I watched too many scary movies, that it was all my imagination. Was it? Because I knew for sure that what I saw this time was not. Mom had been there, in that corner, just hours earlier. I just couldn't find any proof of it.

I slept in that same room each night that week until the funeral was over, hoping she would return, but she never did. I continuously replayed that evening in my head. She said she was okay. That was good. But I was still baffled about the comment that she would take care of me. What did it mean?

One of the many aspects of the spirit world that I have learned about since then is that the messages they relay to us are not necessarily answers to past issues, short-term problems, or something that might happen in the very near future. Often we have to hang on to those messages in our minds and hearts for quite a while and wait patiently for their meanings to materialize. Here in our world, everything we do each day is based on time — when we sleep, when we eat, when we work, when we play. We have calendars and appointments. We check the clock dozens of times daily. But it is my belief that in the spirit realm, time does not exist. Something I am told now by a spirit could refer to something next month, next year, or years down the road. As I would eventually learn, Mom's message about her taking care of me just needed some earthly time to develop — and it involved, of all people, my dad.

The day she died, I called my dad to tell him. His reaction was not at all what I expected. Considering how much he and Mom despised each other for so long, I thought he would be mildly happy or, at the very least, indifferent toward her death. But instead, he cried. In fact, I would say that in subsequent days and weeks he even slumped into a bout of depression. There were probably two reasons for that: one was that he felt some remorse for keeping me from seeing my mom for so long; the other was that he knew her death was tied to her addiction, something the two of them shared for years. Dad also knew deep in his heart that while he may have saved me from the poisonous environment I was in when I lived in New York, what he provided for me in Las Vegas and California was not much better. I think that is why, within a few weeks after I returned home from the funeral, Dad began his journey toward quitting his drug habit. It wasn't something we ever talked about, or something he asked for help with. And it took him a while, probably a year, to fully overcome it. But he made the effort, stuck with it, and to this day is clean.

I ultimately realized that this must have been what Mom meant when she said she would take care of me. Her death had such an impact on my dad that he straightened out his life, which cleared the way for me to live, for the first time, without the stress and anxiety that the two of them had always inflicted upon me with their destructive habits and negligence. Mom had struggled mightily to take care of me when she was alive, but found a way to turn that around in death.

Jump ahead a few weeks, to a Saturday afternoon at the end of that summer. I was back in Southern California and coping pretty well since losing Mom. Some friends and I were walking along a strip mall when we passed a psychic shop. Places like that were all over the region, though I had never paid any attention to them. I actually thought they were kind of creepy.

But as we were strolling past this one, the psychic came out and grabbed my arm to stop me.

"Wow!" she said in an astonished tone. "You have an amazing gift."

I looked at her like she was out of her mind. "I what?" I replied.

"You have an amazing gift," she repeated, looking all serious and moving her hands in the space around me as if she felt some sort of supernatural energy. "You should be doing what I'm doing."

"Okaaay," I said. I looked over at my friends who, by their grins, were enjoying that she picked me to solicit rather than them. Oddly enough, though, she did not immediately try to coax me into her shop and ask me for any money, which was what I thought "those people" were all about. She simply seemed compelled to share her insights.

"But the thing is," she continued, "it's going to take you about three years to understand what I'm saying."

Haha! All right, I'd heard enough. With that outrageous comment I politely thanked her, walked away with my friends, then burst into laughter with them when we were around the corner and out of her sight. I had an amazing gift, but I wouldn't understand it for three years? How did she live with herself churning out such nonsense?

I'll admit that her words did make me reflect on one thing: the night my mom visited me after she died. That was certainly an extraordinary spiritual experience, one that I still had not been able to explain. But as far as I was concerned, I had had nothing to do with it. That was all my mom. I didn't have some "amazing gift" that contributed to that happening.

Or did I? Almost exactly three years later, in October 2002, soon after my eighteenth birthday and because of some inexplicable feelings I'd been having that something supernatural was going on around me, I reluctantly decided to put myself to the test.

I couldn't believe it myself, but the strip-mall psychic was absolutely right. I had an amazing gift.

The Unknown Sister

My father died many years ago, when I was just five years old. My memories of him are fleeting. At the suggestion of a friend, I had a private reading with Bill in 2012 to try to connect with my dad. What transpired from my reading was the most exhilarating story of a broken family reunited across three generations.

Bill knew nothing about me or my family history, yet within a few minutes of my introduction to him, he knew right away who was coming through – it was Dad.

Dad wasted no time sharing his message with me. "You, your brother, your Aunt Cristy – it's like your lives were put on hold after I died," Bill told me Dad had said. "You need to know that I left the planet, but I never left any of you."

To hear this was an enormous gift, far better than any memory I had of the short time we'd spent together here on earth. If the reading had ended after just those first few minutes, I would have been perfectly content. But Dad was just starting. He talked more about my Aunt Cristy (his sister) and my grandmother (his mother). He urged me to visit my grandma, who lived more than a thousand miles away. I hadn't seen her in a very long time. Though I didn't need any more proof that it was Dad coming through, he continued to feed Bill information about my family that couldn't have been more accurate. Until he brought up Susan.

"He's trying to tell me about someone named Sue…or Susan," Bill said.

"I have no idea who that is," I replied.

We went around and around, talking about Susan for a while, and got nowhere. But Dad wouldn't let it go. "It's something you're going to want to remember," Bill said. "This Susan person is pretty important to him."

About two months went by, and then one afternoon my Aunt Cristy called me out of the blue. "Lisa," she said, "I got a strange call today from a woman who claims she is my sister." To give you a little family history: after my grandparents had my dad and Cristy, they divorced. My grandpa then married another woman, my grandma married another man, and each had more children. Cristy and I assumed that if this person who called her was legit, she must have been a half sister we never knew about.

"Nope, she said she's my sister, exact same parents, and has the birth certificate to prove it," Cristy said to me.

With those words, I was overwhelmed with a very warm sensation inside because...well...I just knew. But I asked anyway. "What did she say her name was?" I asked my aunt.

"Susan," she said. I smiled as the warmth intensified.

"Cristy," I said, "I'm pretty sure she's your sister. And there's a guy I know named Bill Philipps, who you *really* need to go see."

As we would eventually learn, Grandma had become pregnant with Susan within weeks after giving birth to Cristy. Dad was four years old at the time. Because Grandma and Grandpa were in the midst of divorcing, and because Grandma was moving in with her parents after the divorce, Grandma's mom and dad had forced her to give Susan up for adoption.

Cristy called Susan back and met with her, as did I, and we were able to confirm that she was, in fact, Cristy's sister and my aunt. Cristy and I then went to visit Grandma, told her what we knew, and arranged for the most heartwarming and emotional reunion between a mother and daughter that anyone could ever witness. Soon after that, Grandma moved closer to the three of us, and she and Susan continue today to meet for lunch and bowling every week.

Cristy did eventually go see Bill, and Dad came through right away. It was an even bigger gift for her than it had been for me, because she and Dad had been in an argument before he died. "It's okay," he told her through Bill. "I'm good, I'm happy, and I love you. I'm just glad that you all are finally together."

To know it was my dad who brought us together – it still gets me choked up. We have three generations of women who didn't know or speak to one another who are now a true family. Bill also gave me the rare and blessed gift of having a second chance to get to know my dad, which I never dreamed would happen. Now I know for certain that any time I talk to him, he is always listening to his little girl.

Lisa

Chapter 2

SEE, I TOLD YOU!

If you choose to see the blessing behind every painful experience, the light of God will heal your soul, giving you the opportunity to help heal others.

When a parent dies, often someone close to the family will graciously and lovingly step in to fill the child's void. For me, that person was my paternal grandma. She actually had been filling the motherly role for me full-time since I was twelve, when I went to live with her. She provided me with the basic necessities every child needs and a ton of love. I hate to think of the path I might have taken without her care, guidance, and discipline.

But I was also fortunate enough to have a second woman who stepped up to help in the later years of my youth: my friend's mom, Rachel. What made Rachel different from a lot of people I knew, including my grandma, was her openness to the possibility of just about anything.

Specifically, in my case, Rachel believed wholeheartedly in spirits. She also believed it was not illogical that someone, even an unsuspecting kid with an unstable past and little direction in his life, could have the ability to communicate with them. When

I was eighteen years old, in 2002, knowing Rachel was one person I could count on to not call me crazy, I revealed to her the experience I had had when my mom visited me three years earlier. The reason I told her was because, for several months, I had been waking up each morning with chills and the sense that my mom was standing next to my bed. Of course, I could not see my mom or anything else to explain it. What I sensed was an invisible presence that, quite frankly, scared the crap out of me. I had the kind of anxiety you might feel if you walked into an old, lightless, abandoned home at night — except I was feeling it every day in my own room, and I had no idea what to do about it.

Rachel, as I expected, was fascinated with my revelation and suggested that I visit a metaphysical shop in Southern California that she was familiar with. "I don't know if they can help you," she said, "but it's as good a place as any to start."

Though I trusted Rachel, I initially resisted the temptation to go, because I had never put much stock in places like that. To me, they were no different than the psychic shop owned by the woman who pulled me aside on the street when I was fifteen, or those services with 1-900 numbers that were advertised on late-night TV and would charge five bucks a minute to have someone tell you your future. Weren't they all scams or intended purely for entertainment purposes? How could anybody possibly tell me what was going on around me when even I didn't know?

The shop was in an outdoor plaza with various stores, and I got as close to it as pulling into the parking lot a few times over several days. I had every intention of going in each time, but I could not get myself to do it.

It's just too crazy, I would think as I talked myself out of it without ever getting out of the car. But this didn't change the fact that I needed advice from somebody. Something was definitely present around me, an inexplicable energy that my intuition told me was triggered by something outside this realm. It wasn't anything ultradramatic. I wasn't seeing dead people. I wasn't talking to dead people. I didn't hear my mom's voice or see her like I did in the bedroom three years earlier. I was just very confused about what I was feeling.

After another sleepless night in late October 2002, the pressure finally overwhelmed me. I drove to the store, parked in the lot, and — after sitting in my car for several minutes — forced myself to get out and go in. I was definitely intrigued when I walked in, but I felt vastly out of place. It just wasn't my thing. It was pretty much a one-stop shop for everything metaphysical. They had books pertaining to the spirit world, incense, candles, and music. You could even get a psychic reading. Coincidentally, on the night I went, they were conducting a two-hour class on developing mediumship skills, the practice of communicating with the spirits of dead people.

Huh, my lucky night, I thought to myself sarcastically. I was exceedingly pessimistic about the chances of my visit amounting to anything worthwhile, and I became even more cynical when the two teachers there stopped what they were doing and gawked at me when I walked in, as if I were a spirit myself.

"Oh my gosh!" one of them exclaimed with an amazed look. "You have such an aura around you!"

They can't be serious! I thought, recalling the almost-identical line from the psychic on the street three years earlier. *Are they all like this? Why in the world did I come here?*

Since I assumed every new visitor was handed that same

phony greeting, and because I was already in the door and would have felt awkward running out — even though I *really, really* wanted to — I just rolled with it. I forced an uncomfortable smile to be polite, introduced myself to them, then grudgingly found a seat in the class while they continued to converse with each other about my "aura."

As I looked around the room, I felt like I was in a bizarro world. The other students were in their forties, fifties, sixties, and even seventies. Some were wearing flamboyant clothing and beads, looking like an outsider's stereotypical idea of a psychic or medium . . . or someone who just stepped out of Woodstock. It looked like a gypsy convention. I didn't know any of them and was way out of my element. I was wearing jeans and a T-shirt, was one of just a few men in attendance, and was by far the youngest one in the room. Everyone else could have been my parent or grandparent. I'm pretty sure one could have even been my great-grandparent. I again questioned myself about why I was there. *It's going to be two hours of pure hell to get through this with a straight face,* I thought.

Not only did I make it through, but I was also forced after the two hours to accept the obvious truth: there was something to what the teachers thought about me, and I could not ignore it any longer. They put me and the others through two tests during the class period, and the results of my tests were undeniable.

One test was in psychometry, which is a form of extrasensory perception, more commonly referred to as ESP. It is the process of connecting to someone or something through the energy of an object. The other test was in mediumship, or connecting with the dead. During the psychometry test, a woman in the class I'd never met before sat across from me and gave me her ring. I held it securely in the palm of my hand, closed my eyes, and was told by the teacher to reveal what I was seeing or feeling. What I saw in my mind was a house, and what I felt was that it was the woman's house. I was able to describe it in great detail — the color, the layout inside, where the trees were in her yard, the vines that climbed the side of the house.

Too easy? Not really, if you think about it. I had no idea why those images spontaneously appeared in my mind. Guessing the color of her house would have been one thing; you have to assume I would have had maybe one chance in six or seven of guessing correctly if it were a typical house color. But I wasn't guessing — I saw it in my mind. And how I was able to perfectly describe everything in and around the house was perplexing to everybody. All those details just because I held her ring? No way!

After the owner of the ring confirmed that all I had said was true, one of the teachers was taken aback by how descriptive and accurate I was. The woman who owned the house looked at me in wonderment, put her ring back on her finger, and walked away speechless. She probably spent that night looking out her window to see if I was stalking her.

Okay, I thought. *That was interesting.* It hadn't convinced me of anything yet, but it had piqued my interest enough to make me want to hang around and see what was next.

We moved to the test on mediumship. It was somewhat similar to the psychometry test but felt much more personal. I was paired with a different woman; but instead of holding an object that belonged to her, I was told to hold her hand. In this case, too, I had never seen the woman before and knew nothing about her. I was again instructed to say whatever I felt or saw, such as any impressions, feelings, or images that came to mind.

I firmly sandwiched her hand between my hands and closed my eyes. The first image immediately popped into my head. "I'm seeing long, blonde hair," I said as I opened my eyes to catch her reaction. "It's a female with long, blonde hair that she keeps brushing back behind her ears."

The woman gave me a blank stare. No expression whatsoever.

I closed my eyes again and took much longer this time, probably thirty seconds or more. I knew what I saw, but was hesitant to say it. Self-doubt is probably the number one obstacle psychic mediums face when first discovering their gift. "I'm seeing the letter *J*," I said. "The initial *J*. Someone close to you whose name begins with *J*."

I opened my eyes. Still no reaction. She didn't say a word. I felt deflated. It was a good thing *she* couldn't read *my* mind. *C'mon! What's wrong with you*, I screamed at her in my head; *why are you just staring at me? Are you not hearing me? Give me something — a nod, a wink, anything!*

I took a deep breath, closed my eyes again, and pressed forward. "A round end table with prescription pill bottles," I said. "They are overflowing, falling off the table because there are so many." As I gave that statement and still got no reaction from the woman, one of the teachers happened to be walking by as she was making her rounds through the room.

"And how could you interpret what you just said?" the teacher asked.

I contemplated it. "Well, I guess the overflow of bottles could point to an overdose of pills," I said indecisively, hoping I was correct.

I was dead on. The woman's hand, which I was still holding, started to quiver uncontrollably. She then burst into tears. I was stunned. *What happened? What did I say?* As it turned out — everything. The woman wiped her eyes, regained her composure, then confirmed every detail I had told her.

"My friend committed suicide from a drug overdose," she said. "She had long, blonde hair and used to always flip it behind her ears."

My jaw dropped as I stared at her in awe. And she wasn't finished. "Her name was Jennifer," she said. The *J* name.

The teacher was astounded. "You really need to look into this further," she said to me after processing what she had witnessed in both tests. "You definitely seem to have the golden link to the other side. Spirits seem to be connecting with you. Keep testing yourself." She then rushed to the opposite side of the room to tell the other teacher what I had just done. Students on that side of the room who overheard her were stopping their readings to look over at me. The amazed looks they all had on their faces were priceless. They were blown away.

So was I.

I hugged the woman I had just read for, but I don't remember saying anything to her. I really didn't know what to say. I still wasn't certain what had just happened . . . or, more important, how it happened. *A golden link to the other side? Spirits? Is that really what just happened?* I thought.

The reaction of the teacher who witnessed what I did has always stuck with me. The purpose of the class was to hone these gifts that people supposedly had, yet the teacher was so shocked by what I did that she couldn't wait to run to the other side of the room to tell her colleague, who was just as enthralled. Maybe it was because it was my first time or because I was so young, but they certainly seemed caught off guard as much as I was. I guess they had seen students in the past display low levels of psychic or medium abilities, but nothing like I had just done — and definitely not on their first try.

I returned for a couple more classes after that to learn more about tapping into whatever it was I had going on, but I didn't get a lot out of them. Not to sound vain after just a few classes, but whatever I supposedly had — a gift, talent, blessing, curse; I still didn't know what to call it — seemed to be in a far more advanced stage than anything they offered to teach me. I also sensed this from the teachers' astonished reactions to what I did in the first class.

I felt, too, that what I had was something natural, much more than what others in the class had or were striving to have. To try to force it in any way by applying lessons learned in a classroom wasn't going to work, in my opinion. If I felt it — whatever "it" was — then I felt it. If I didn't, then I didn't. That opinion was probably triggered by the fact that the spirits are the ones in charge, not me. I didn't think of it in that context at the time, because I still wasn't sure what was going on or who was behind it all. But I had a gut feeling that whatever it was, no class was going to dictate its direction.

When I went back to Rachel after that first class and explained what had happened, she reacted as I expected: not at all surprised, and extremely excited. "See, I told you!" she said. But Rachel wasn't completely satisfied. Wanting to encourage me further, she asked me to do a reading for her.

Uh-oh. The thought of doing that made me uneasy. Taking what I had discovered within the walls of a metaphysical shop — among people I had never met and would probably never see again — and testing it with someone I was very close to was awfully intimidating. What if it didn't work? What if I upset Rachel in some way? I felt there was too much potential for something to go wrong between friends. But on the flip side, I knew it was the only way I would find out if this "connection" I appeared to have was truly real, or if what had happened in that store was an anomaly. And who better to test it with than the person I trusted the most with this?

My reading for Rachel, on its own, ended up proving nothing. But I was forced to do an additional reading, with someone connected to her, that not only verified the legitimacy of the reading with Rachel but also took me and this ability I had to a whole new level. I knew after the second reading that, like it or not, I really did have an incredible gift.

For my reading with Rachel, I followed the same routine as in class, since I didn't know any other way. I sat across from her and closed my eyes while holding her hand. In a matter of a few seconds the images instantly appeared, one after the other, and much more fluidly. It was as if those two initial readings in class had smashed open a gate that had been holding the spirits back. They were charging through like bulls on the streets of Pamplona. But one spirit in particular pushed his way ahead of the others and took charge of the reading. I had a sense that he was someone who had recently taken his own life. That was followed by images of a gun.

Rachel kept a straight face, like the woman in the class, as I gave her this information. I kept going. "I see a red pickup truck," I said. "And now I'm hearing something about someone named Michael and the city of Sacramento."

That's when I had two major breakthroughs in this *golden link*. One was that I had just *heard* a message rather than *seen* an image. I didn't hear another voice — I heard only mine. But it felt as if my inner voice were acting as a messenger for a spirit. I didn't see an image of Michael or Sacramento; I heard those words. In a later chapter I will explain more about the spiritual senses — the *clairs* — including clairvoyance (seeing beyond the human eye) and clairaudience (hearing beyond the human ear). It was a fascinating discovery.

Even more fascinating, though, was the second break-through: I felt as if Michael, whoever he was, was actually the spirit inside my head! *He* was the one who took his own life. *He* was the one giving me all these signs and messages. They weren't just *about* him, but *from* him! The term *spirit* was no longer just a general term — there was an actual deceased person behind it. The only way I could describe it at the time was that there was something about that moment in my mind that felt so personal, so powerful, as if the voice of my consciousness were not the only voice present.

For now, just understand that these were two revelations that would give me an entirely different perspective on what I was capable of doing, in addition to a more personal relationship with the spirits going forward.

What Michael was so urgently trying to tell me was that he wanted to get a message to someone — not to Rachel but to someone named Kimberly. "He wants Kimberly to know that he is okay," I said with more confidence than I had previously felt during a reading. "He also wants her to know there is a box of letters he wrote to her that will reveal how much he loved her."

The reading ended there, when I felt Michael had left and was not giving me any more information. Rachel gave me a few nods during the reading, but showed no other reaction. I was puzzled. The woman in the class held in her emotions before letting them out at the end, but Rachel wasn't even doing that. As she explained when we talked about the reading after it was finished, that was because none of what I said was personal to Rachel in any way. She couldn't think of anyone she knew named

Kimberly, at least not someone in the present or from the recent past. And nothing regarding Michael — not the truck, the gun, or even Michael himself — meant anything to her.

Rachel didn't think for a second that I was off track; she just didn't know, at the time, the significance of anything I had said. She took notes throughout the reading and told me she would hang on to them and review them later.

I felt discouraged. Not so much because I'd failed to prove I had some special power or gift, but because my reason for exploring what was going on around me in the first place — that uncomfortable and unknown energy I was feeling that I thought was my mom — was producing no concrete answers. In fact, everything now seemed even more convoluted. How did I go from feeling that energy around me at home to such precision in the two class readings, and then to not even being in the ballpark in Rachel's reading? But I knew what I saw and felt. The images and names that had infiltrated my mind were vivid. If they meant nothing, then they meant nothing. I could not change what came to me. But I still had no answers. What on earth was going on with me?

It took several days, but I finally found out.

Rachel was in her home office about a week after the reading when a new client came to see her — a client named Kimberly. Rachel was an accountant and was going to be working on Kimberly's taxes. The reading hadn't even crossed Rachel's mind when Kimberly set up the appointment. As they started going through the forms, Rachel asked Kimberly if she had any dependents to claim. Kimberly looked at her, got choked up, then broke down and cried. She said her son had recently passed away. Rachel still had not started putting the pieces together. She asked what the son's name was.

"Michael," Kimberly said.

I've always pictured that moment as being, for Rachel, like the scene at the end of the movie *Field of Dreams* when the catcher takes off his mask and Ray Kinsella, played by Kevin Costner, is stunned to see that the catcher is his father, who had died many years earlier. Once that mask was removed and Kimberly and Michael were identified, Rachel realized she was in the midst of an incredible drama that was only going to get more interesting as she unraveled it.

Brimming with excitement, Rachel calmly excused herself from the meeting for a moment and ran to her bedroom to grab the notes from our reading. When she came back, she delicately asked Kimberly some questions about Michael and compared Kimberly's answers to the notes.

Cause of death? Gunshot.

Where? In his truck.

Color of the truck? Red.

What city was he in? Sacramento.

It all checked out with 100 percent accuracy. Kimberly was floored when Rachel showed her the notes.

"Who told you all this?" Kimberly asked, shaken that a stranger could know any of it.

"His name is Bill Philipps," Rachel said with a soft smile, explaining to her who I was and what I did. "Don't worry, I'll make sure you get to meet him."

The letters that I had mentioned in my reading with Rachel remained a mystery, though. Kimberly said she and Michael had gotten into an argument before his death and had not spoken in a long time. She knew nothing about a box of letters.

A couple of days later, I met Kimberly at Rachel's house to give her a reading. Kimberly seemed nervous, for obvious reasons, but was anxious to hear what else I could tell her. What happened transformed both of our lives.

With Michael's spirit coming through as strongly as it had during my reading with Rachel, I was able to lead Kimberly to the girlfriend Michael had lived with before he died. In that girlfriend's house, in the back of a bedroom closet, was a box of letters he'd written to his mom during his personal struggles. The letters revealed how much he loved his mother, and that he wanted her to know what a wonderful job she had done in raising him, despite their falling out. He obviously never mailed the letters, and his girlfriend had no idea the letters were there.

Kimberly had come to Rachel simply to get her taxes done, but she left with something far greater than any refund check could have provided: the knowledge that her estranged son was at peace — with her, and with his life on the other side.

Those readings with Rachel and Kimberly gave me tremendous insight into how spirits work. I learned that giving a reading to a person does not mean that what will result is meant for that person. The spirits have the power to orchestrate unusual meetings between people, including people who may not even know each other, in order for the spirits to communicate their messages to their loved ones. Michael wanted to get a message to his mom. He knew that I, as a medium, would be receptive, but first he had to find a way to connect us — two people whose paths had never crossed. He used Rachel, someone he and Kimberly did not know, to make it happen.

Pretty electrifying, isn't it? I see it happen almost every day now, and I'm still staggered by it.

I also learned a couple of other things from what transpired with Michael, Kimberly, and Rachel. One was that a message from a spirit could take time to decipher, just as my mom's message to me that she would take care of me took me a while to figure out. The other was that the primary purpose of a spirit's attempt to reach somebody is generally to let that somebody know he or she is okay in death. I did not fully grasp that right away, but my connection with Michael was another example of it, just like when my mom told me she was okay.

While I knew this gift I had was absolutely substantial, I was still struggling to find my way with it. This wasn't like having a calling to embark on a traditional career. Some people are destined to go into sales or marketing. Others may feel like engineering is in their future. Some may be called to become mechanics. I was starting to feel like I was being pulled to a life of relaying messages from the dead. I don't think a career aptitude test has ever generated that as a possible profession.

The class at the metaphysical shop and the readings with Rachel and Kimberly all happened in October 2002. I had graduated from high school the previous spring and had been taking some general studies classes since August at the local community college. I was also taking voice lessons. I wasn't a typical singer, a kid who could simply carry a tune well enough to entertain people. I was blessed with a rare operatic tenor voice, one that very few teenage boys — or even adults — had. I had used the voice in my high school choir and in school plays and had been thinking that music, at some point and in some way, would become my career.

But the spirits seemed to be telling me otherwise. Unsure

of what direction to take, I compromised by doing it all for the next two years. I attended classes at the community college, took voice lessons, and did whatever I could to keep my intuitive abilities well tested and sharp, such as giving readings when time permitted. I didn't like spreading my life so thin, but I knew it would only be temporary. Something would have to eventually rise to the top.

Across the Miles

When I found information about Bill on the internet, I was hoping he could connect me with my father, who had died suddenly many years earlier at the age of thirty-nine. Bill was in California and I was in Florida, so we did the reading over Skype. As soon as Bill appeared on my computer screen and introduced himself, I laughed. *My gosh, he's just a kid!* I thought.

But, as I quickly learned, he was a kid with a gift unlike anything I'd ever seen. Within the first couple of minutes, Bill said my dad and grandma were coming through. He gave me several validations to prove it was them, but then he took the reading in a different direction when he said another spirit was present. "It's an *L* name," he said. "A Laura, maybe. No, Lorraine. I think it's Lorraine."

I was shocked for a couple of reasons. One was because Bill was able to come up with an uncommon name like Lorraine. The other was that Lorraine was the name of my stepmother in California, and I had not spoken to her in years. My dad had married her after a messy divorce from my mom. I'd lost contact with Lorraine after my dad died, and I had no idea she had passed.

"Lorraine says she and your dad are fine – she is taking care of him like she always did," Bill said. "And your dad wants you to know that he's sorry for what happened between him and your mom."

Bill then paused for a moment.

"And do you have a stepsister?" he asked. "He and Lorraine really want you to get back in touch with her."

I couldn't believe what was happening. Bill was giving me a perfectly accurate account of my family, assuming Lorraine had actually died. As we were about to disconnect, he said that one more spirit was fighting his way through.

"Sean...or maybe John," he said. "It's a short, one-syllable

40

name." I had no idea who that was. It certainly wasn't anybody in my family.

"It will probably make sense later," Bill said. "I think at this point, the most important thing is to reach out to your stepsister."

When the reading was finished, I called my stepsister, Sheila. She told me she had been thinking of me recently and was glad I called. We talked for a long while, and she confirmed for me that her mom, Lorraine, had died about six months earlier. But I didn't know if I should tell her about Bill and the reading. What if she didn't believe in that kind of thing? Our reunion on the phone was going so well that I didn't want to mess it up. But as we talked more about our family, I felt compelled to tell her. I told her everything Bill said, including the information about a John or Sean.

Shelia fell silent.

"Is something wrong?" I asked.

"Sean is my son!" she cried.

Sean had died several years earlier in a car crash in which she was the driver. Though it was purely an accident, she had carried a heavy burden of guilt since his death. I teared up as she told me the story of what happened. I realized that maybe the reading I'd had with Bill wasn't meant for me, at least not solely. Maybe the spirits who came through to me orchestrated everything so that, ultimately, Sean could get in touch with his mom and help her heal. "You know what, Sheila?" I said. "I think you are supposed to meet with Bill."

Shelia didn't live far from Bill, and she set up an appointment to see him. She said that when she arrived, Sean's spirit was already waiting there for her. He told his mom that he was okay. He said it had been his time to go, and she should feel no guilt for what happened. He was happy, and she needed to be happy, too.

As I traced what had happened – how I found Bill, how Dad and Lorraine and Sean found me, how I found Shelia, how Sean and Sheila found each other – I was in awe of how it all evolved. Bill managed to bring a family that had been separated for decades back together. He provided all of us with an amazing comfort that we would not have experienced had he not connected us with the other side.

I still say Bill is just a big kid, but he's a big kid with a rare and astonishing gift that connected my family on this side with my family on the other side – something I hadn't imagined was possible.

Mary

Chapter 3

A MEDIUM (with YOUR) LATTE?

Trust that you are here for a greater purpose; let your
light shine and guide you. You don't need to know your
destination…just take the first step!

Oh yeah, there was also a fourth thing on my to-do list:
work close to forty hours a week as a barista at a café. I
was a poor kid out of high school who had to somehow pay for
college and voice lessons, so I squeezed as much work as I could
into each week. I usually worked enough hours to make it nearly
a full-time affair.

So, college, voice lessons, testing my gift when I could, and
a full-time minimum-wage job. After just a few weeks, I was
functioning on little sleep and was exhausted beyond measure.
I knew it was going to be a struggle to keep up that pace. The
physical demands, which ranged from the strain on my voice to
being on my feet all day at work, were draining. They also contributed to my overall mental fatigue, which made it difficult
to concentrate while testing my intuitive skills. My sanity was
being pushed to the limit.

But none of that discouraged me from wanting to do it all.
I just needed to find a way to manage it efficiently and remain

effective. That's when my creative side kicked in. I decided to combine two of my tasks into one. No, I didn't bellow Mozart's *Le nozze di Figaro* while whipping up a medium latte. That would have just been weird. Trying to use my psychic abilities on customers while taking their drink orders, on the other hand . . .

One pertinent piece of advice that I recalled the teachers at the metaphysical shop giving me after I read for those two women in class was that I should frequently test myself to see how deep this gift went. I equated it to learning a new language. You can learn all the words and conjugations from a book or tape or teacher that you want, but you will not become fluent in that language unless you practice it regularly in your everyday life. I needed to challenge myself by conversing with others to see just how good I was at it.

Since I had little time to do readings of any significant length, one way I kept sharp was by trying to determine the names of customers at work whom I'd never seen before. The purpose of this test was not just to see what percentage of names I could get right but also to learn to trust my gift and the internal messages I was receiving from spirits. If I was receiving messages from them, but not trusting what they were telling me, then what was the purpose of the gift?

The test was a fairly simple one. I would focus on the person I wanted to name, then listen for an inner voice from a spirit — the same inner voice that had enabled me to receive messages from Michael when I was reading for Rachel and Kimberly. More to the point, I was silently asking a spirit to telepathically send me the name of the person I focused on. Sometimes all I would get was an initial, while other times I would receive an entire name. Occasionally, the spirits were not cooperative and I would get nothing. But nearly every time, they were there for me.

I would do this exercise while customers were standing in line. So I might pick out a young woman, concentrate on her, silently ask a spirit for her name, write the name down, then try to inconspicuously find out her name when it was her turn to order. I would usually introduce myself in a way that would trigger her to tell me who she was. "Hi, I'm Bill," I would say in the friendliest possible tone and with a smile that filled the room. If she gave me a beaming smile in return, I'd playfully say, "And you are . . ."

"Emily," she might reply. More often than not, I got the name right. If I didn't, I was usually close. By "close," I mean instead of Emily, she may have been Emma. Or instead of Ann, she may have been Anna. Even if a guy was named Robert instead of my guess of Ronald, or Walter instead of Wayne, I was pretty satisfied with the attempt.

If I was completely wrong, like not even in the ballpark, there were usually a couple of explanations. Often I would find that the next customer in line, or someone else in close physical proximity to the person whose name I was trying to figure out, had the name I had written down. It was a case of one spirit getting in the way of another spirit. For example, the spirit associated with Emily may have been there front and center, but a spirit for Anna — the next person in line — may have stepped in front of the spirit for Emily, causing me to write down Anna's name instead. As I'll discuss later, this is a common issue in my readings that can create some confusion and take a little time to straighten out. One spirit will be running the show, then another one suddenly pops in. They can be a bit pushy with each other at times.

Another explanation for the wrong name was that the name I received was in fact from a spirit connected to the person, but the name was that of the spirit and not of that person. So, for example, let's say I believed the woman I was serving was named Heather, but her name was actually Rose. After striking up a conversation with Heather, I might find out that Rose was the name of her mother, who recently passed away. So the spirit, Rose, was giving me her own name, not her daughter's name. When the spirits communicate information to me, especially names, it can get tricky. The name could be that of the spirit, of the person the spirit is trying to connect with, or even of someone else — living or dead — who has ties to both of them, such as a significant relative or friend. It is all part of the validation process, as I later discuss in greater detail.

Of course, I always kept this test to myself. One reason was because I was at work and didn't want to disrupt my coworkers. The other reason, of course, was because it probably wouldn't have been a good business practice to scare the crap out of the customers by telling them their names before I served them.

Because that overall experience produced such positive results for me, I continued to put myself to the test on the coffee shop circuit. During what little free time I had, I started frequenting a small café near Rachel's house. I know... who stops at a café for leisure when he already puts in nearly forty hours a week at another one? But since I visited Rachel often, it was a short, easy, comfortable stop on my way to see her.

As a customer there, I tested my abilities on other customers who were sitting near me. Here too, I tried to figure out their names, wrote them down, then struck up conversations to see if I was right. I also tried it on some of the waitresses — except that as I got to know most of them, I admitted to them what I was doing. Fortunately, they didn't freak out on me. In fact, their reactions were quite the opposite — they wanted more! They would have friendly battles over who got to serve me, hoping I could give them quick readings during their stops at my table. It meant great service for me — I'd never been to an establishment where I was asked so many times if there was anything I needed.

As weeks went by, other customers started asking me about my gift; the waitresses had been spreading the word. The next thing I knew, I was giving readings to other customers — and some of them were voluntarily paying me for them. In fact, they didn't just *want* readings, they were practically *begging* me for them. Not only was it not my intention to make money off my experiment, but the thought never even crossed my mind. I was still in such an early stage of developing this gift and had done so few readings that I could not imagine confidently thinking I could gain a client base. But it happened, and quickly.

Customers would perk up the second I walked in, and they would ask me to sit by them. As I left, they would ask me when I was coming back and would try to plan their schedules around mine. I think I became a bit of a novelty to some at the café. They would expect me to be able to tell them what they did that day or where they were heading next. Some would even bring in their friends to see if I could tell them their names. That's when my use of this gift started to go beyond the coffee shop.

People there would ask me to meet with them privately to give them in-depth readings without the distraction of so many people sitting around us or a waitress constantly checking on us. They didn't want only the quick insights that I could give during the time it took me to drink an espresso — they wanted full-blown readings like I give today. They were so captivated by what I could do that word spread swiftly throughout town. Now I was even busier than before — I had school, voice lessons, and a job, and was giving lengthy, detailed readings to people outside of work in the few spare moments I had.

In January 2003, just a few months after I had started working at the coffee shop, I decided to give my two-week notice. It's not that I wanted to — I liked my job a lot and still enjoyed the simple challenge of trying to figure out the names of customers in line (it was also a great way to meet a lot of new people). But with the demand for readings on top of everything else I was doing, I simply couldn't focus on what I needed to do when I was supposed to be doing it. I was spread so thin that I was feeling stressed, which of course is not healthy, no matter what's on your plate. With the readings providing the income I needed in order to pay for college and voice lessons, it made sense to leave the coffee shop and continue honing my gift. It was time to take it to the next level.

The Unlikely Connection

My mom lived on a beautiful ranch on the Northern California coast and always seemed so happy. But unbeknownst to anyone, she had long been silently suffering with depression. The pain was so deep that in the spring of 2011, she took her own life. I was her only child. Losing her was devastating, to say the least.

Before meeting Bill, I had seen a few other psychic mediums. Some were legitimate. Some weren't. I decided to give Bill a try when a friend, who knew I wasn't coping well with the loss of my mom, referred me to him. The reading was done over the phone. He didn't know who I was or even what I looked like. I was hoping that wouldn't hinder his ability to give me at least a sliver of comfort.

Many mediums I'd been to struggled with names, but Bill picked up on my mom's presence immediately and knew everything about her — her name, how she died, where she had lived, what kind of dog she had owned. It was uncanny. "She wants you to know she is sorry for what she did," Bill said. "But she says it was time for her to go. She is in a good place."

The reading continued with one validation after another, when suddenly my mom was interrupted by another spirit. "I'm getting a J name now," Bill said. "A relative or friend with a J name. He ended his life the same way your mom did."

I had no idea who he was talking about. I couldn't think of a J name close to me, let alone someone else who committed suicide. Where was my mom? Why was this J guy getting in the way of my connection with her?

"Who is Paul?" Bill blurted out of nowhere.

"Paul?" I asked, even more confused. This was getting out of hand.

"Yes. Paul is here now. He is somehow connected to this J person," he said convincingly.

And that's when it hit me! My partner, Maria, had a brother named Wilfred who had changed his name to Jason. He had taken his own life about twenty years earlier, soon after his partner, Paul, died of AIDS. I knew of Jason and Paul but had never met either one, since I'd known Maria for only six years. You could have pushed me over with a feather at that point. I couldn't believe the connection Bill had made.

"But how could this be?" I asked. "My mom never knew Jason and Paul. I didn't even know them."

"It doesn't matter," Bill said. "Once they are on the other side, they know the connections they have with each other in relation to you and those you know. Jason and Paul helped bring you here today so that you can let Maria know they are okay and happy. It's also another validation from your mom that it's really her speaking to you."

What Bill provided for me that day changed the course of my life. I had been deeply depressed after losing my mom. I had sought help in various ways, but nothing and nobody had been able to give me what Bill provided. No pastor, no psychologist, no one — and for one simple reason: I believed in my heart that Bill was truly speaking directly with my mom at that very moment.

I was raised with a strong faith in God and heaven, and what Bill did was strengthen that faith. I know some people think the work of mediums is the work of the devil. I understand that concern, but it's inconceivable that someone who provides the love and compassion that Bill does can have a connection to anything evil.

Because of that one reading, I no longer suffer from depression. I no longer think about my mom's death each day. Not only have I been able to move forward with my life, but I also have been able to do it with a level of happiness that I never thought I'd experience again.

Shelly

Chapter 4

THE HAUNTED HOUSE

The universe/God/Spirit is always available and eager to help in any situation – but you must be willing to ask for that help, then have faith that it is on the way.

The demographics of the clients who began seeking me out for readings varied widely: they were men, women; college students, middle-aged, elderly; blue-collar workers, business owners...and of all races and socioeconomic statuses.

I had no website or office at the time. I eventually spent about ten dollars to purchase plain white business cards printed with nothing more than my name, phone number, and the words "psychic medium," but that was the extent of my advertising budget. All my business was generated by word of mouth. It started at the coffee shop near Rachel's house and extended to the teachers at the metaphysical shop, who referred their students to me. Friends of mine were telling their friends, who told their friends, who told their friends. I was booking multiple people a week without any personal effort, doing readings in their homes or in public venues that might afford us a little bit of privacy, like in a park or at a corner table in a restaurant. Readings for groups of people at house parties on weekends were common. Instead of hiring a musician or disc jockey for an evening of entertainment, hosts were hiring me. The demand was beyond comprehension.

But despite my rising popularity, I had two things working against me. One was the fact that I looked every bit the nineteen-year-old college student that I was. As Mary in Florida said when she first saw me through Skype, which was described in an earlier story, I was "just a kid." One time I walked into a house party I'd been hired for and was mingling with the guests before my reading, when somebody asked when the psychic medium was going to arrive.

"That's me," I said proudly.

"Oh," she said with a disappointed tone. "I thought you'd be older. . . and a woman."

Well, that was a lovely greeting. What young man doesn't like to be told that he should have been an older woman, and in front of a bunch of people he doesn't know?

The other strike against me was that people were naturally skeptical of anyone whose job title had the word *psychic* in it — the same way I used to be. Go ahead — take whatever your job title is and put the word *psychic* in front of it. Your credibility just plummeted, didn't it? Can you even do it without laughing?

"Hi, I'm Elizabeth. I'm a financial adviser." Cool! Here is my money for you to invest for me, Elizabeth!

"Hi, I'm Elizabeth. I'm a psychic financial adviser." Uh, yeah, I think I'll keep my money under my mattress.

Of course, being called a "medium" wasn't much better, but at least it was a softer-sounding word that hadn't been abused as badly by the street scammers who called themselves psychics and gave people false hope after taking their money. But I was who I was. I couldn't hide from it, nor was I motivated to start a worldwide movement to make people stop saying "psychic" and start saying "clairvoyant" or "visionary."

I quickly learned, after a few successful readings and several tremendously positive reactions to my work, that there was only one way to break those stereotypes: by conducting a spectacular reading each time that would prove I was no act. So that's what I did.

One reading that stands out from that period was for a woman named Melissa in Southern California. I went to her home after she had witnessed me in action one afternoon at her friend's baby shower (hey, don't laugh — think about it next time before you drive yourself insane trying to organize those silly baby-shower games). She lived in a townhouse, and we were downstairs sitting at her dining room table. After some casual conversation, I felt a spirit present. Suddenly, something happened to me that had never happened before.

"Whoa!" I blurted out, jerking my body backward. "I feel like I just got hit by a train." It was as if the wind had suddenly been knocked out of me. I wasn't immediately sure what had happened or why, but as I would find out over the course of our reading, it was my first time experiencing clairsentience — the ability to physically feel a spirit. The significance of that moment was enormous. Previously, clairvoyance and clairaudience had been the only ways spirits had communicated with me.

What was fascinating after it happened was that Melissa seemed more intrigued by what I said than by the fact that I nearly fell out of my chair for no apparent reason.

"You said *train*," she noted with a look of concern.

"Yeah, that's what it felt like," I replied. I stopped her there.

Before she could say anything else, I closed my eyes because I could sense that the spirit who had nearly knocked me over was trying to tell me something.

"I see a couple crossing a railroad track," I said. It was a man and woman, with the woman on the man's shoulders. But it did not look like Melissa.

"They're laughing. . . but something went horribly wrong. I see limbs on the ground," I said. It was a disturbing image to reveal, but the presence and determination of the spirit were so strong. "Were they hit by the train?"

When I opened my eyes, Melissa had tears rolling down her cheeks. I wanted to ask her what was wrong, but the spirit was still powerfully coming through and wasn't finished. Had Melissa been crying hysterically, or if she had asked me to stop, I would have stopped. But she wasn't and didn't, so I kept going.

"I feel like the woman died, but she wants you to know she is okay. . . that it was quick and painless. She said they were drinking and just being stupid, but that she wants you to know she is at peace."

Melissa said it was like I was there that night.

"That night" was a few years earlier, when Melissa and some of her friends were barhopping near San Diego. They happened to run into the same man and woman in a few of the bars. Even though Melissa and her friends did not know the couple, they all drank and played pool together throughout the evening. Melissa and her friends decided to stop at one more bar heading home, while the couple decided to go elsewhere. When Melissa exited that last bar, she spotted the man and woman, with the woman on his shoulders, crossing the nearby railroad tracks and laughing loudly.

She also saw a bright light and heard a horn — from the train barreling toward them.

The woman fell forward off the man's shoulders, onto the track, and . . .

The gruesome incident that Melissa witnessed never left her mind. The part most disturbing to her was that she had made direct eye contact with the woman before the woman was hit. It was an eerie connection in the very last moment of that woman's life. Melissa had never talked about that night with anyone. She knew there was nothing she could have done to prevent the tragedy, but there may have always been a slight sense of guilt in her subconscious, since she had been drinking with the couple just before the woman's death.

But after my reading, Melissa was at peace. "For her to communicate that she was okay was good closure for my soul," she later told me. The emotions Melissa had instantly shown when I said the word *train*, and when I told her what the woman was saying, indicated how much that incident had affected Melissa's life and weighed on her mind. The calming words from the woman's spirit enabled Melissa to release that negative energy and free herself from any guilt she felt.

I found through that and other readings — and, more important, my clients found out — that my readings were not just something fun to do. I was bringing people incredible peace and healing and hope and, sometimes, as in Melissa's case, closure. They may have initially brought me in as entertainment, but more often than not I left most of them in tears — tears of joy and relief spontaneously released when they made a connection to the other side.

As my reputation as a peacemaker and healer continued to expand, so did the number of requests people made. In particular, I was starting to receive a fairly substantial number of calls from homeowners who claimed their houses were haunted. They wanted to know if I could help them get rid of the spirits.

That was entirely new territory to me. I had never encountered a haunted house, nor was I sure how my gift would play into that, if at all. Yes, I connected with spirits, but they came to me — I did not go to them. They also did not appear to me in a form that I could outwardly see or hear, which was my understanding of what made a house a "haunted" house. The spirits in my daily life appeared in my mind, and very peacefully. They didn't scare me. There was nothing haunting about them. The word *haunted* is unfavorable in itself, stirring images of fear and distress. That was not what I, or any spirit who had communicated with me, was about.

I initially turned down those homeowners' requests. They just never felt right. But as the calls continued coming in, and as I gave the idea more thought, I realized the possible connection to me. Fear and distress were what a lot of my clients in individual readings were experiencing and the reasons why they sought my help — fear and distress about where their deceased loved ones were, the negative terms on which they had parted, or unfinished business between the parties before the person died. Melissa had wanted a reading done with no specific agenda in mind, yet the distress she had felt from an incident years earlier disappeared after my reading. Maybe there *was* something I could do about a haunted house.

The lucky person who called me with a haunted house problem while I was considering this issue in a new light was a woman in Southern California. It was early in 2003. Her house was built on a cliff overlooking the ocean. It was a beautiful home, but it was also rather ominous since she said spirits were lurking inside. She said several doors in her home, in which she lived by herself, were slamming randomly and at all hours of the day.

I'll say this: if I lived alone and doors were slamming for no apparent reason, I'd probably sprint out of there rather than bring someone in.

"Do you think you can help me?" she asked when she called.

"Probably not, since I have never done this before," I said frankly, "but I will certainly give it a shot."

I expected that when I got there I would be given a tour of the house, no doors would slam, and the experience would be lackluster at best. Why would the spirits risk making themselves known to me? But here's what actually happened: When I walked through the front door and into the grand foyer, I instantly felt the forceful presence of two spirits. Chills and vibrations coursed throughout my body, as if an icy breeze were passing through me on a dreadfully hot day. The sudden energy made me nervous. Had I not known the house was haunted, I probably wouldn't have been as concerned. But knowing these spirits had been bothering the homeowner, I wasn't sure how they would react to an outsider such as me, or what they might be capable of doing to me — especially if they knew I had been called there specifically to deal with them.

"I can already feel something," I said. "Did a man and a woman used to live here?"

"Yes, they owned the house before I bought it," she replied.

"Did they both die here?" I asked.

"Yes," she confirmed.

And that's when information from the two spirits of the previous homeowners began to flow into my mind. We were still standing in the foyer when I saw an image of a piano, but there was no piano in the foyer. Only a chair, couch, and small table stood there now.

"I'm seeing a piano," I said. "Do you have a piano in the house?"

"Oh my gosh," she said, surprised at my question. "No, but there used to be one right where you are standing. This was their piano room. We knocked this wall down over here and got rid of the piano at the same time."

I sensed right away that this was one of the problems. "They want their piano back," I said with a slight grin. "They don't like what you've done with the place."

"Seriously?" she said.

"Yes, seriously."

But I also knew that unless one of the spirits was Liberace, this had to go deeper than the absence of a piano from a room that had been redecorated. And even that wouldn't explain why the spirits were still in the house and not on the other side. "I feel like one of them committed suicide and one was ill," I said. "Do you know how they died?"

"Well, you're exactly right," she said, appearing stunned by my knowledge. "The husband died of cancer...he was pretty young. And I was told that his wife was severely depressed after he died and that she jumped off the cliff in the back."

And there it was. Don't ask me how I knew, because I'm not sure myself. But I just knew. Intuition, I guess. "They haven't crossed over," I said.

"What do you mean?" she asked.

"I mean they're still here. They're dead, but they're still here."

"So they're... ghosts?"

"I guess you can say that," I said. "They died, but they are still connected to this house. It probably has something to do with them dying so suddenly. They weren't prepared to go."

And then the fun really began. Almost right on cue, doors upstairs began to slam. We both jumped. "Is there anybody upstairs?" I asked the homeowner. *Please say yes! Please say yes! Please say yes!* I repeated in my head as my stomach turned.

"No," she said.

Of course not.

After the last door slammed and everything was peaceful for a few seconds, there was a crash in the kitchen. We both hustled in to find a painting that had been hanging over the stove now lying on the floor. There was no way it could have randomly fallen, and at that precise moment. This wasn't going well.

"Please, what can you do?" she asked with desperation. "I can't live here like this anymore!"

Once again, call it intuition, instinct, a hunch, a good guess . . . I told her to get me a candle and a match and to lead me to a dark, quiet, comfortable place within the home, assuming there was one left. She took me into the living room and drew the blinds as I lit the candle and began to meditate. This wasn't a light meditation where I was just trying to calm myself down after what I had witnessed and felt, though I certainly needed that. This was a very deep rumination. I held my hands out with my palms up and envisioned a bright white light — my vision of heaven. I told the two spirits to go to the light and let it lead them wherever it would lead them. This wasn't a séance, in which someone chants or says something else out loud. It was all done in my mind in a very low-key fashion. I was trying to communicate with the spirits in the same way they communicated with me.

After about fifteen minutes, when the energy level in the room felt like it had dropped, I opened my eyes and looked at the homeowner, who appeared to have an expression of relief on her face. She knew something good had happened. "Are they gone?" she asked.

"I think they are," I said. I wasn't feeling their presence anymore. I didn't actually see them go to the light as I had encouraged them to do, but I had a good sense that they had gone. At least everything was quiet in the house for the moment. "Time will tell," I told her. "But I feel pretty confident that you'll be alone now."

I checked in with her a couple of weeks later, and there were no outward signs of any spirits. They never bothered her again.

"I can't believe it," she said. "How did you do that? And how did you know to do that?"

The only explanation I had for her, and the only explanation I still have today, is that I let my intuition take over and be my guide. Quite honestly, I didn't know what the heck I was doing. If you want to say I was lucky that it worked, I can't argue. But I can tell you that my instincts told me that meditation was the thing to try.

How exactly did I meditate? My first step was to surround myself, the house, and the two spirits with white light, or what I specifically envisioned as the light of God. I knew that the light of God was all powerful and would cause all negativity to vanish. I know it sounds a little eerie, but it was very simple and, apparently, very effective.

While I did that, I let the spirits know that I was listening to them, and that I was guiding them and giving them permission to leave the home and follow the light.

You are dead, I told them. *You need to leave. This is not your home anymore. You need to go to the light. It will take you to a place of peace and happiness.* I didn't chant it or do anything creepy that you might see in an old black-and-white movie. I tried to be conversational, but direct.

So why did they not go to the light as soon as they died? I think it was because they didn't know for sure that they were dead. They were earthbound spirits, or ghosts, and didn't know what was going on. How does that happen? I believe when people die tragically, some of them feel cheated out of their "contract" with life here on earth. They feel as if it isn't yet their time to go, so they take longer to cross over, possibly even needing help to do it. If someone is murdered, she might be "stuck" here on earth in the form of a spirit. Her body is dead, her soul has left the body, but the soul is confused. She doesn't know she is dead, or isn't ready to be dead, and feels like she has unfinished business here. "You want to knock down a wall of my house and get rid of my piano?" I could envision one of them saying. "Not while I'm here!"

How many times have you heard of a house being haunted after someone who lived there died peacefully, and died at a time in her life that made sense, such as during old age? Hardly ever. Most people who claim to live in a haunted house find that the person who used to live there died suddenly and in a shocking manner or at a very young age. The person was not ready to go and may not even have known that her life had ended.

How, then, was I able to help the spirits escape this dimension and cross over? One word: communication. What I believe makes a house haunted is that the spirits, who don't know what is happening, are competing for the same earthly energy that you want. It is your house now, but they still believe it is their house. While they cannot be seen or heard, their actions — such as slamming doors or knocking a picture off the wall — can be seen and heard because the doors and picture are earthly things being moved by the spirits' energy.

And what do we as humans generally do when doors start inexplicably slamming and things fall off walls? We run. We run out of fear, and as far away from the situation as we can. (As I said, that would have been my natural reaction if it were my house.) And then when we come back, hoping the spirits have left, it starts all over because we are in their space again. Or if we move out of the house, then the next family has to deal with it, which is why a house might be haunted by the spirit of someone who died decades or centuries ago. Rarely, and for good reason, do we stay put and compassionately say, "Okay, how about if we talk this out? Let me explain to you, whoever you are, what is going on and where you really should be right now. Let me help you get out of this predicament."

I communicated with the two spirits in the woman's home very clearly, through my mind, the same way spirits communicate with me. I told them it wasn't their house. I told them they were dead. I told them where to go. And they listened. Will that always work in a haunted house? I have no idea, because I never tried it again.

After that highly charged day that sucked every ounce of energy out of me, I decided it would be the last haunted house I would try to "unhaunt." Going forward, I would stick to communicating only with spirits who had crossed over. While what I did was a success, it was too emotionally, spiritually, and physically draining. The drama was too much and, quite frankly, it spooked me. When you walk into a house for the purpose of ridding it of a negative energy, and that energy attacks your senses by slamming or crashing things around the house, it gets your adrenaline going and the situation becomes intense. Experiencing it once was enough for me.

Even the Cat Was Involved

I first met Bill many years ago through a friend of mine. My husband, children, and I have had several readings from him since then. Back when Bill wasn't as popular and as inundated with reading requests as he is now, he would make house calls. One day I called and said we needed him to come over as soon as possible. When he walked in the house, I didn't even have to tell him what the issue was. He could feel it.

"There is definitely energy from spirits here," he said.

A couple weeks before Bill came over, I had gone into the kitchen one morning and noticed the coffee pot was already on and brewing – but nobody else in the house was awake, and there was no automatic timer on it. In the days that followed, lights turned on and off by themselves and water ran even though nobody had opened a faucet.

And then came the most exciting moment: when I woke up in the middle of the night to find our fifteen-year-old cat, Sherlock, running through the hallway, jumping up and down and meowing as if he were carrying on a conversation with someone. He'd never done anything like that before, and it seemed especially uncharacteristic in his old age.

Bill said all those things were happening because there was a spirit in the house who hadn't crossed over yet. After spending some time with us, he determined that the spirit was Richard, the brother of my husband, George. Richard had died a few months earlier. He had been a prankster, and to hear that he was responsible for flicking the lights and starting the coffee pot was no shock to anyone. But why would Richard hang around? Just to be funny?

"He's concerned about George," Bill said. George was overweight, had diabetes, and also had some heart issues. Bill said Richard wasn't comfortable leaving George in that condition.

After Bill's reading – to appease his brother and to get our home back to normal – George went on a special diet, exercised, and nurtured himself back to good health. At one point during George's transformation, we noticed nothing was being tinkered with anymore. I went to Bill for another reading and he told me that Richard had indeed finally crossed over. He said Richard was happy about what George had done, and that there would be no more disturbances.

You may have noticed earlier that I said what happened to the cat was "exciting." I used that term because there was nothing at all scary about what Richard was doing, even before we knew it was him. What happened was intriguing, more than anything else. I mean, c'mon, even the cat was involved! But I'm happy to say that thanks to Bill's insight, George got healthier, Richard finally crossed over, the house settled, and Sherlock was able to sleep through the night undisturbed.

Diane

Chapter 5

SPIRIT HOMEWORK

Your loved ones are always with you in spirit. The more you recognize their presence in subtle ways (through nature, music, thoughts), the more they will validate their presence, and the more at peace you will be.

After that haunted house incident in early 2003, I got back on track with my normal readings — in quiet and comfortable locations where positive energy ruled and doors weren't being abused. Every reading I did — no matter who it was for, how long it lasted, or what resulted from it — increased my knowledge, in some way, of my gift and the extent of my capabilities. It was like doing anything else in life: the more you practice it and experience it, the more you learn and the better you get at it. Sometimes I discovered new psychic or medium skills. Other times I learned there were things I couldn't do or shouldn't be doing. I also learned a lot about the spirits — how they communicate, what they expect of me, and the best ways to relay their messages to their loved ones.

It was important for me — and still is — not only to review each reading and harvest any new lessons or knowledge that I could but also to do these things as soon as possible after the reading. The reason for the urgency is that it is difficult for me to retain what happens in each reading. I don't mean only that it's difficult to remember one that happened last month; sometimes it's also hard to recall one that I did yesterday or even this morning.

When I give someone a reading, I'm in a zone. It's a trance-like state. My focus is completely on the spirits and the client, and I tune out everything else around me. The spirits rapidly throw information at me, and I dispense it to my client as it comes in. It's like music passing through a radio signal to a listener. The client and I then talk about it and interpret it, a lot of emotion is expended by both of us, I briefly reflect on the reading, and then I have to disconnect from it so that I can mentally prepare for my next reading. To do that next reading, I try to completely forget the previous reading and start anew. The slate needs to be clean so I can focus on the new client and the right spirit or spirits intended for that client. For me to recall details of each reading, especially when I'm giving multiple readings a day, nearly every day of the week, is just too much. I have to continually discard files or my mind will crash from the overload of information.

And yet some readings stick with me no matter how much time passes, because of who the reading was for, the reaction of the client, or the unique quality of what transpired during the reading. An example of that is the one involving the train and Melissa — the first time I ever experienced clairsentience. Another one occurred in the fall of 2003. It has stayed with me because it involved my childhood friend Michelle and a friend of hers who was new to me. It also provided me with a lesson I now call "spirit homework."

✴

Michelle was a big believer in my gift. I had read for her once previously and it had gone very well, but this second time was much different, because, unfortunately for her, very little information that pertained to her materialized. I could feel multiple spirits in my mind throughout the reading, but one was clearly louder than the others, overriding anything the others were trying to push through. I could tell it was an older man, a grandfather possibly, but it was not Michelle's grandfather. He brought up the word *Dakota*. I knew he wasn't referring to one of the states. It felt like someone's name.

"A friend I work with is named Dakota," Michelle said.

Bingo! That was easy. Dakota was such an uncommon name that I was certain it was her. When Michelle went back to work a couple of days later, she started a conversation with Dakota about grandparents. That's when Michelle found an opening to ask her if her grandfather had recently passed away.

"Yes, about nine months ago," she said. "Why?"

Now came the difficult part. "Well . . . my friend Bill is a medium," Michelle said. "And while he was giving me a reading, I think your grandfather was trying to communicate with us."

Dakota was born and raised in a devout Catholic family. Mediums fell outside of her religious convictions. For Michelle to tell her that her dead grandfather was trying to reach her was preposterous on the surface, but Dakota was intrigued enough to continue listening.

"If you want to meet with Bill, we can find out for sure if it is your grandfather," Michelle said. "If not, then we'll know the spirit intended to reach someone else."

Though Dakota was extremely skeptical, her curiosity was piqued enough that she saw no harm in meeting with me to see what this was all about. Later that week, Michelle and Dakota met me at a restaurant for lunch. We exchanged hellos, shook hands, sat down, and were instantly joined by a fourth party — Dakota's grandfather. This guy didn't waste any time.

"So my grandfather has been talking to you?" Dakota asked with a grin.

"Yes, and he's already here," I told her.

Her grin disappeared. She didn't expect something like that to happen so soon. We hadn't even looked at our menus yet. "So he's here? With us right now?" she asked.

"He is," I said. "Give me just a moment." I looked down and closed my eyes to get a clear vision of his message.

"He says he hears you praying to him when you are in the car," I said.

Dakota's eyes welled up. Talk about a home run on the first pitch during the first at bat.

"You're kidding me," she said softly, trying to keep her composure. "I . . . I talk to him every morning in the car on the way to work." She unrolled her silverware from her napkin and used the napkin to pat her eyes. "I always feel like he's there with me, listening to me, even though I can't hear him."

"He *is* with you," I said. And as if that weren't enough validation for her, Grandpa hit another home run during his next at bat.

"I'm not sure what this refers to, but he wants me to tell you that he does not like your music," I said.

Dakota's jaw dropped as she laughed.

"One day last year I borrowed my grandpa's car and put my CD in," she said. "I forgot to take it out, and he had no idea how to work the CD player, so he listened to that CD for a week until I saw him again." It was a moment they both joked about for a long time afterward.

Her grandfather gave me a few more stories to share with her, providing Dakota with unwavering validation that it really was her grandfather who was with us. "He says he just wants to let you know that he is happy," I said.

That would have been the perfect ending to another heart-warming and successful reading. A grandfather coming through to his granddaughter, creatively using his granddaughter's friend to reach her, and wanting nothing more than to let her know he is in a good place. But that's not at all how it ended.

As happened during my reading with Michelle that brought Dakota and me together, and as I've mentioned previously, several spirits are usually in my mind fighting to get themselves heard. Once that door is open — once I am focused and giving a reading to a person or group — it can become a free-for-all as far as the spirits are concerned. The most determined ones will maneuver their way to the front of the line. In this case, Dakota's grandfather said what he wanted to say. Then he was pushed aside by another spirit who also wanted to get a message to Dakota.

"Hang on a second," I said to Dakota, interrupting her euphoria over the fact that her grandfather had come through. "I'm getting someone else here . . . was someone in your family murdered?" I asked her. Talk about a 180-degree spin.

"What? No," she said, bewildered by the question.

"Hmmm . . . yes, somebody was murdered," I insisted. "I'm seeing the numbers nineteen and twenty-four. Maybe he was nineteen to twenty-four years old?"

Dakota didn't just give me the blank stare that I'd often received in readings when people didn't know what I was talking about. She gave me a cold, hard glare and proceeded to tell me how wrong I was. The happiness her grandfather's spirit brought her had flipped like a switch to anger. "Nobody in my family was ever murdered!" she snapped.

"Well, I'm not sure who this is, but he says he knows who you are and he is trying to let you know that he too is okay," I said. I closed my eyes for a few seconds and asked the spirit if he could identify himself. Dakota and Michelle were silent as I did this.

"His name is Daniel," I said. "He was killed. It was some sort of head trauma that happened in front of a lot of people." This visual was getting ugly. I wasn't liking it any more than Dakota was, but I knew this was a good spirit who was just trying to identify himself in a way that she would understand. Daniel really wanted her to know that he was okay. The problem was that we had no idea who Daniel was.

"Listen, I know my family!" Dakota fired back at me. "We have no Daniel and nobody was murdered. You're wrong!"

I felt horrible that I had stirred such negative emotions, especially after the reading started so well for her, but as in my reading for Rachel about Kimberly that made no sense at the time, I could not deny what was coming through to me. He was trying to reach Dakota — there was no doubt about it.

The spirit, who was possibly sensing the tension he created, left. We ate our lunch without a whole lot of conversation, because the strain of the reading still simmered. We parted ways politely, and it was over. . . at least on my end.

When Dakota got home later that evening, she called her mother to tell her about the experience. She felt compelled to tell her about her grandfather coming through, since he was the father of Dakota's mother.

"It was pretty amazing that he was able to tell me things that nobody else could have known," Dakota told her mother, "but I'm not so sure what to believe now. After that, he told me someone named Daniel in our family was murdered."

Her mother gasped. "What else did he tell you about Daniel?" her mom asked.

"What? Why? What's wrong?" Dakota replied, suspecting her mom knew something that she didn't. Her mom paused to gather her thoughts.

"Dakota, have you ever heard us talk about my cousin Spike?"

"Yeah, I think so," Dakota replied.

"Well, his real name was Daniel. He had been involved with a gang and was shot at a party. I was there," her mom said.

Dakota was tongue-tied while her mom continued to confirm my reading piece by piece. "He was shot in the head," her mom said.

Dakota felt overwhelmed as the bits of information I'd shared with her during the reading rattled through her brain — Daniel, murdered, head trauma, happened in front of a lot of people. And then came the clincher, as if Dakota needed one at that point. I had told her that the numbers nineteen and twenty-four had come through. My interpretation was that maybe Daniel was between nineteen and twenty-four years old. But the numbers were even more specific than that.

"Mom," Dakota said, nervous about asking the last question. "How old was Daniel when he died?"

"Well, let's see," her mom said. "I was nineteen, so that would have made him . . . he would have been about twenty-four."

That last answer solidly verified both that the spirit was Daniel, and that it was actually Dakota's mother he was trying to reach. He wanted to tell his cousin, the one who was with him the day he was killed, that he was at peace.

Needless to say, Dakota is one of my biggest supporters

today. And she not only is still true to her religion but also says that what I was able to convey to her actually strengthened her faith by affirming there is a life of eternal rest and happiness after this one. She knows without a doubt that her grandfather and Daniel are in heaven.

I call revelations such as the one about Daniel "spirit homework," and it was a significant lesson in the early stages of my discovery and development of this gift. While most people I read for expect to immediately understand or recognize what I am telling them, it doesn't always work that way. You'll remember that was the case in my reading with Rachel. I told her about Kimberly and Michael, but it took a week for her to find out who they were. Rachel's homework was easy: someone named Kimberly came to Rachel, Kimberly told Rachel about Michael, then Rachel verified with Kimberly everything I had said. It was like giving a kid an assignment with the answers attached to it.

In Dakota's case, the assignment was much more difficult. She should have taken the information I gave her and done some homework to see if there had been anyone named Daniel in her family, before drawing the conclusion that nobody in her family had ever been murdered. But I don't blame Dakota for her reaction. Keep in mind that this was not a reading she initially sought — she agreed to it because of what Michelle told her about her grandfather. Dakota may have been a little bit prepared for information from her grandfather — but she certainly was not ready for Daniel. None of us were.

If you were to come to me for a reading, hoping to get answers to pertinent issues in your life, it would be useful for you to know that answers don't always immediately emerge, no matter how much you want them to. It is a lot like prayer. When you pray to God for something, your prayers are rarely answered on the spot. It would be nice if they were, but that's not how God works. If someone you love is ill, it can take days or weeks or months of continuous prayers before they are answered.

Spirits work in similar, mysterious ways. For that reason, you should not dismiss anything in a reading that doesn't make sense to you. Instead, accept it and consider it to be homework. You may need to do a little research outside of our reading, or be more aware of your surroundings, to find the answers you want, but chances are very good that they will eventually materialize.

Friends on the Other Side

I once went to a well-known psychic medium to see if she could make contact with my deceased husband, Doug, who had died of brain cancer. She told me that he was healed, that he said to say hello to his brother...and that was it. Ninety-nine percent of everything else she fed me had no connection to him whatsoever. It was a total waste of time.

Soon after that disappointing reading, I heard about Bill and decided to give him a chance. It took him less than five minutes to top what the other medium had done over the course of an hour.

He started out a bit vague, asking me what significant person in my life had an *R* name. I assumed that meant my current boyfriend, Randy. Everyone probably has a significant *R* name in her life if she thinks long and hard enough about it, right? But it was just the beginning of a convincing road Bill led me along toward my husband.

After mentioning a few other minor, but certainly possible, validations, Bill got specific. "Who is Wayne?" Bill asked. "Your husband says he is with a friend named Wayne."

Here is the thing about Doug — he was a loner. He had very few friends. I was generally his only outlet. But when we used to go to Wisconsin on vacation to visit my girlfriend and her husband, Doug and her husband made a connection. His name was Wayne. He died of skin cancer six months before Doug died. "He was so quiet that I'm surprised he even found Wayne," I told Bill.

"Actually," Bill said, "it's not just Wayne he found. They are both with another person, too. Someone named Bill."

I definitely didn't know anyone who passed named Bill, and I knew Doug didn't either.

"Do some homework on that one," Bill told me. "Keep it with you, and I bet you'll find out who Bill is."

He was right, and it took me less than a day. After the reading, I called my girlfriend to tell her about Wayne being with Doug. During our conversation, I remembered that Wayne's brother, too, had recently passed, but I couldn't remember his name.

Of course, it was Bill.

There were other revelations throughout the reading about other members of my family that Bill Philipps nailed – but telling me that Doug was hanging out with Wayne and his brother was really all I needed to hear. I guess I assumed that when we cross over, we drift right to our family and remain close to them all the time. And Bill did say that Doug was with others too, including his mother and my mother. But it was Doug's connection with Wayne that astounded me.

Bill told me that Doug and Wayne were going to continue hanging out together, at least until my girlfriend and I get up there to join them. I have no idea how long that will be, but it's pretty cool to know that Doug has found himself a good friend to be with until I get there. It's such a peaceful and calming feeling to know that in my absence someone is with him to keep him company and take care of him.

Sue

Chapter 6

COMING out of the CLOSET

You have all of the ingredients for success. Honor yourself
by knowing that you have what it takes. Success comes from
within.

ife for me continued on the same steady path for the next
year, but I knew it couldn't stay that way for much longer. My
dad and grandma were both hounding me about doing something with my life, and they both fully expected this "something"
to involve singing. Sure, the readings were going better than I
ever imagined; I was making a lot of people happy with them,
and I was able to support myself at the same time. The problem,
though, was that my dad and grandma had no inkling about that
side of my life. I purposely never told them.

I never told them about my mom appearing to me, about
the class at the metaphysical shop, and about quitting my job at
the coffee shop to spend more time focusing on readings. There
was just no way I could...especially Grandma. My grandma
was a devout Christian and read the Bible almost daily. I knew
she would not only discredit my claim that spirits were communicating with me, but she would also be very angry that I had
become involved with anything like that. I figured my dad would

take a more casual approach and just tell me I was a nut job. I lived with both of them, which made it even more remarkable that I was able to keep that side of my life a secret for so long. Now you know why I never had a home office in which to conduct my readings, and why I had to meet people like Dakota in a restaurant.

In October of 2004, with my voice stronger and more developed than at any point in my life, thanks to two solid years of lessons after high school, I was offered the extraordinary opportunity to audition for enrollment in the prestigious San Francisco Conservatory of Music. I was one of about one hundred prospective students trying out for a few open spots in January 2005.

Based purely on numbers, my odds of getting in obviously weren't very good, but I had to try. Why couldn't I be chosen? The truth was that I really wanted to try out because I loved to sing and had been working so hard for so long at perfecting my craft. As a bonus, the audition also gave me a reason to delay saying anything to my family about the readings. If I didn't make it into the school, then I would worry about what to tell them. At the very least, the audition was going to buy me some time.

The conservatory's history dates to 1917. It is a specialized school that trains you for a performing career in classical music. The student body represents more than two dozen countries. The curriculum is well rounded, though the primary focus is obviously on music study and performance. Instead of math, you would take music theory. In addition to Western civilization, you would study music history. It is not a school where you go to discover your talent; you have to have an extremely high level of talent to even be considered for admission. Then that talent is honed to prepare you for a life in that field of study. And I found that being born with a rare and exceptional voice can certainly help your chances of getting in.

My voice stood out among the other candidates' voices during auditions, so much so that I was offered an open slot. I would eventually be identified as a young heldentenor, someone with a rare dramatic voice that lends itself to the operas of Wagner. I was viewed as someone with an incredible amount of potential, someone who, with age and a lot of hard work, would succeed in the world of opera.

How could I refuse such an opportunity? It was the chance of a lifetime and what I had been working toward for so long. In addition, Grandma and Dad were both ecstatic about it, which made me happy. So I accepted the school's offer and headed 450 miles north to the beautiful Bay Area in January 2005 to begin my new life. It also meant that I still didn't have to say anything yet to Grandma and Dad about my other life, which I figured would be placed on the back burner anyway with school now my primary focus.

But I still had one major problem: the spirits came with me to San Francisco.

I know I didn't invite the spirits to join me, but I should have known by then that where I go, they go, invited or not. I guess I thought they might cut me some slack, knowing the colossal venture I was about to undertake — but then again, I wonder now if they stuck with me because they knew how much closer my education at the conservatory would actually bring me to them. As I would soon find out, the conservatory not only honed my gifted voice but also coincidentally sharpened my skill as a psychic medium in a couple of ways.

One way was through the vibration of the music, which was very similar to the feeling I had when tuning into spirits. We all know that music alters our moods and can play a huge role in our daily attitudes. Let's say you're having a bad day, you flip on the radio, and one of your favorite feel-good songs comes on. That song lifts your energy. Singing along with that song also lifts your vibration, from a negative vibe to a positive one. You may walk around all day carrying a lot of grief and emotional junk that you just can't shake, but the vibration of music can break through that junk and let your light shine. For me, a psychic medium, the vibration emitted by music connects my energy with my soul, inducing an incredible euphoria that raises me up and can join me more easily with the spirits. Spirits reside in a high place — much higher than ours — where the vibration is at a very high level. When bridging our two worlds, the spirits lower their vibration, while I raise mine. The vibration of music has taught me how to effectively raise my vibration so that the spirits and I can meet somewhere in between our worlds and communicate with each other.

A second way the conservatory sharpened my skill as a psychic medium was by training me to perform in front of audiences. Singing at the conservatory is a highly difficult mental task. I had to practice four hours a day in a small officelike cubicle with faculty listening to and criticizing every sound I made. The grind became depressing at times...not much different from any other job where you sit in a cubicle all day and have to listen to your boss tell you everything you are not doing correctly...except I wasn't getting paid. Then, every so often, I would have to sing on stage in front of them. And when I got on stage, I felt free, relaxed, comfortable. Even though I was still being heavily critiqued, the environment of a magnificent open stage versus a tiny drab cube was day versus night. I was taught that to sing on stage, I needed to "breathe and trust myself," a technique I use all the time as a psychic medium. I could not do the readings I do in front of large crowds today if I were not at ease in front of them. The conservatory helped me immensely in that respect.

When I got to the conservatory, I cut back on my readings considerably. Since I had been accepted into such a prestigious school, and they were taking a chance on me over so many other qualified candidates, I wanted to swap my priorities. I limited my readings mainly to people back home, those who already knew I was doing them. I did most of them by phone and some when I went back home on breaks. That approach enabled me to focus on school, earn some spending money on the side, keep my senses sharp, and keep the spirits happy. And it all went very smoothly for about a year. Until I was outed.

A girl I knew from Southern California who was accepted into the conservatory the year after I got there told some people about my gift. I never told her not to, so I couldn't really be upset with her. Then again, I never expected someone from hundreds of miles away who knew about my gift to be accepted into the same exclusive school that I was. The chances were so slim, but it happened.

As word spread, fellow students were stopping me in the halls of the school each day, asking me if I talked to ghosts. Many of them had smirks on their faces when they asked, as if they had a joke cued to fire at me if I said yes. So I told all of them the only thing I could tell them: "What? No! Are you out of your mind?"

I did that on the advice of my voice teacher, a very spiritual woman who was the only person at the conservatory whom I had personally told about my gift. She implored me "to deny this gift to anyone here who asks. They won't understand."

The previous semester, before I told her about my abilities, she had been swimming while on vacation in Hawaii and was knocked down hard by a wave, resulting in a broken arm. She returned to the conservatory in a cast, able to use only one hand on the piano. As she was giving me a lesson one day, I got the feeling that I was supposed to tell her my secret. During a short break, I told her I needed to share something with her. "I'm not sure why I'm telling you this or how you'll take it," I said, "but I want you to know that I'm a medium."

I guess you could say she took it pretty well. She jumped up from the piano, nearly stumbled over her seat, and cried as she gave me an enormous hug. She said she had been asking God to send her someone to emotionally help her because the accident and recovery had been so traumatic for her. We bonded at that moment unlike anytime previously. That was when she told me not to tell anybody else.

After that, we spent time together outside the conservatory talking about metaphysical phenomena, and I also gave her readings. She was so gripped by what I was able to do that she said she wanted to help me enhance my abilities as a medium as long as I was a student there. As much as I wasn't convinced that I should accept her offer, because of its potential to distract me from my singing, she presented it in a way that made her feel like an ally, someone who would understand me and not judge me. I put my trust in her and, just as she promised, she helped propel my gift to yet another level.

She boosted my abilities by creating three simple strategies for me. The first was to continue keeping it a secret from everyone at school, denying it whenever necessary. "You don't want students talking about you or it will only hinder your confidence level," she said. She told me most students were too young and naive to appreciate what I could do. She thought most of them would see me as a sideshow — someone to entertain them on weekends when they were bored — rather than as someone who might be able to help them improve their lives. She didn't want them to abuse my gift or distract me by making fun of me, or for me to be afraid of being ridiculed in class each day.

The second strategy was for her to teach me to "sing spiritually." She coordinated all the different chakras — various energy points in the body — with the way I would sing. It taught me to visualize each chakra being opened as I sang a certain vowel sound. I know, you are probably thinking *chakra*? It's very complicated, and difficult to put into easy-to-understand terms. Even a glance at an online description of what it is doesn't simplify it much. But what she did was correlate the way I sing with the energy inside me — going back to what I talked about earlier with regard to the vibration of the music opening up my connection with the spirit world.

The third strategy, once we had built a strong relationship and trusted each other, was to gradually tell certain people about my gift. Not just anyone at the conservatory, but specific faculty she knew at other colleges and people in opera around the world whom she knew would be open to my gift. And it worked. By the time I graduated from the conservatory in May of 2008, my primary clientele for readings had changed, from friends back home to high-level opera people across the United States. For example, one was an opera singer from the East Coast. Her husband, a world-famous tenor, had passed away, and I was able to connect her with him multiple times. I told her that she was eventually going to move to San Francisco and teach at the conservatory. She didn't see how that was possible. The only thing more difficult than getting into the conservatory as a student was getting in as a faculty member. But about six months later, after a faculty member was unexpectedly fired, she was contacted to fill the position and she accepted the job.

Just weeks after I graduated, at twenty-three years of age and with my gift flourishing, I made a bold decision: to pass on pursuing a career in the field I'd just spent the previous four years studying so that I could turn my side job of communicating with the dead into a full-fledged career. Honestly, it wasn't as difficult a decision as I thought it would be. I think I had felt for years, as I was working toward my degree, that I *had* to be a singer. It was the normal thing to do, and I did have a passion for it. But connecting spirits with people had gradually become my true passion.

Readings often felt like work in the early years. There was always an uncertainty inherent in them that made me nervous. What spirit would come through? How would the person I was reading for react? How would I handle the messages coming through? Where would I do the next reading so that my family wouldn't find out? But I didn't want to hide it anymore. I felt so alive when I did a reading. It was a rush. I felt an elevation unlike anything else, even unlike the sensation of singing opera in front of an audience.

My singing might affect someone's life for the moment, but my readings were changing lives forever.

Of course, if this was going to be my career, I had to come out of the closet and reveal what I had kept secret from so many for so long. I had a website built by early September and sent an email blast to my family and closest friends, including some of those at the conservatory, explaining what I was going to be doing. The response I got was overwhelmingly positive. Among the students at the conservatory I previously had lied to about my gift, not a single one made fun of me once they got to experience firsthand exactly what I could do. I remained in the San Francisco area for about a year after I graduated, so I was able to give readings for students, for faculty, and for friends of students and faculty, bringing a lot of peace to a lot of people. My clientele list was growing mightily. I was doing multiple readings a week and could not escape the endless requests. As time-consuming and exhausting as it was, I felt I needed to do it for as many of them as possible. I felt a responsibility to honor my gift — and not just at that time but permanently.

The reaction from my family and friends in Southern California was just as encouraging. Many of my cousins were excited for me. I had an aunt who called to tell me how proud she was of me. Even people who weren't sure what to believe with respect to the spirits were happy that I was happy.

The only two people not a part of that email blast were my dad and my grandma. I knew I needed to tell them face-to-face. When I went home and told my dad, his reaction was swift and clear: he said I was the devil and a fool for not pursuing singing. That was difficult to hear because he was my dad, but it didn't sway my decision. Given the life he had led, I expected a little more compassion from him. His reaction really didn't make sense to me, but I understood the emotions he felt.

As for my grandma — well, it didn't sit well with her, as one might expect. She heard me out, though it changed nothing about her opinion of what I was doing. Again, I understood. But I still knew I was making the correct decision. The irony was that she was the one who taught me about Jesus, a healer and instrument of love and peace who was persecuted simply for who he was. He didn't change who he was or what he stood for because people disagreed with him or his methods. No, I am not saying I am Jesus, or that what I went through in making my decision to share my gift was in the same realm as what Jesus went through. Please don't think that for a second. What I am saying is that while growing up, I was taught by my grandma, as many of us are taught by our parents or guardians, to be like Jesus. I was taught to spread love and peace, to look beyond those who might harass me for what I knew was the truth, and to be courageous about it — knowing that I was doing the right thing.

I had a unique gift, and I wasn't making a rash decision about what to do with it. It had been nine years since Mom had appeared to me, and five years since I first realized for certain what I had. I felt a responsibility to use this gift to bring happiness and harmony to the world, no matter who disagreed with me or tried to bring me down.

All Bets Were Off

My wife and I were in the San Francisco area one weekend in 2009 to watch my alma mater, UCLA, play football. On our drive home, we stopped to see Bill. My wife had told me he was a medium, and that her sister had made an appointment for them to see if Bill could connect them with their father. That was the extent of my involvement – and my interest. I didn't ask her any questions. I was just tagging along.

When we got to Bill's place, I sat in a chair at the back of the room, barely paying attention to them. Bill had no idea who I was. Not my name. Not my background. Not my relationship to the two women seated in front of him. There were no introductions.

I didn't enter the session completely unwilling to accept what I might see or hear. I simply intended to be a neutral observer. While I do believe there is some greater energy in the universe that most of us are not able to access, I also believe that 95 percent of the "fortune-tellers" or mediums out there are parasites trying to take people's money. Bill's odds, from my perspective, weren't good.

I am a well-educated man who is skeptical by nature and by job training. I'm a partner in a Northern California law firm and serve as a pro tem judge. I have been in this line of work for nearly thirty years. In essence, I spend my work hours ascertaining when people are lying so I can filter out the real stories and expose charlatans.

I expected Bill to start the same way I'd seen a couple of mediums on television conduct their readings – by asking my wife and her sister a lot of leading questions, which he would then use to "guesstimate" what had happened in their lives. But that's not how it played out at all. He didn't ask them a single question. The first words he spoke were that he sensed a presence, "a father figure."

A moment later he said that a second father figure was in the

89

room — a "father-in-law," he said. My wife and her sister looked at each other…then all three of them looked at me.

"What?" I said incredulously. "Wait…time out. I'm not in this." I wondered why he was trying to rope me into this thing. But I quickly realized he wasn't. My late father was.

"He's showing me a green tractor," Bill said. "He's a farmer, sitting on his tractor at his farm."

My jaw hit the floor. How could a guy who had no idea where I was from, what my name was, or that my dad had recently died, call out a guy in the back of a room in the heart of the Bay Area, where farms are scarce, and know that, yes, my father was a farmer and had a green tractor? With that, all bets were off. And Bill was just getting warmed up.

"He really wants to communicate with a woman, but she's not in this room," Bill said. "He has a deep love for her. His wife. He's showing me a K name. Is your mother's name Kathy?"

My jaw was still firmly planted on the floor. I was so paralyzed that I didn't know if I could even say yes. My father, through Bill, went on to perfectly describe the scene in the hospital before his death. Though he had been in a coma, he knew that my mom had been holding his hand. He knew everything she had said to him. He even mentioned the pact.

My parents were so much in love that they had made a pact years earlier that they would die together. I was their only child and knew all about it. Dad told Bill that he was upset he didn't keep his end of the bargain, and that my mom should go on with her life until they could meet again on the other side.

The skeptic's mind asks, "How did Bill know all this? Where did he get this information?" This lifelong and professionally trained skeptic determined there was only one logical answer: my father told him from the other side.

I totally expected that going to the UCLA game and meeting up with my old college buddies would be the highlight of our weekend in San Francisco. It was — until I unexpectedly got to meet up with my dad.

Steve

Chapter 7

SPIRITS and FAITH

Part of the process of finding your spiritual truth is keeping the information that resonates with you and leaving the rest behind. Trust your feelings, and know that the most important place to find God is within you!

I try not to mention anything about my work as a medium when I'm around my grandma, since she disapproves of it, but I felt such a strong presence from a spirit one day several years ago when she and I were at home that I couldn't help asking her about him. I felt like he had a tie to each of us, but I had no idea who he was. I thought she might. I don't normally bring up spirits with anybody who doesn't want me to, but I felt this unknown spirit was as much a part of my life as he was of hers — as if there was a blood connection.

"Hey Grandma, did you know someone named Tim?" I asked. "A younger guy, maybe in his early twenties? Someone you never got to say good-bye to? Someone maybe related to us?" I knew nothing about my family history, so the name didn't mean anything to me. But it did to her. I struck a nerve.

"How did you know that?" she asked sharply.

"How did I know what, Grandma?" I replied, trying to draw some information out of her about him.

"I had a cousin named Tim," she said. "He went missing when he was twenty-one. We never found him."

"I can feel him," I told her with as much compassion as I could muster, hoping she'd open the door, a little bit, to who he was. "He is here with us."

But she quickly slammed the door shut as she shot me an incredulous look. She knew that I knew something, and I could tell she wanted to say more, but she would have none of it. She darted into the other room to get her Bible while loudly repeating "No! No! No!" convincing herself there was no way Tim was present with us. Out of respect for her feelings, I let it go.

A Bible is always in close proximity to Grandma. Because of her religious convictions, she does not eat meat. She prays constantly. We always prayed together before meals when I was growing up. She used to turn on Bible-based cartoons when I was little. She is "old school" in many ways when it comes to her religion. She has led a very honest and truthful life and is a good person, one I have no doubt has a comfortable spot reserved for her in heaven. And as the Bible tells her to do, when it comes to communicating with spirits of the dead, she avoids it.

She has always felt that the devil has a hand in what I believe is my God-given gift. She believes not that I am the devil, as my dad once suggested, but that the devil is tricking me and using me by posing as spirits to infiltrate the lives of others. In other words, if I tell you that your grandpa is coming through to me, she would say it's really the devil pretending to be your grandpa so that he can have easier access to your life. The Bible says, in a nutshell, that mediums are supposed to be avoided for that reason. But given my countless positive, firsthand, daily experiences with spirits, I don't think the issue is so black-and-white.

✳

I truly believe God gave me this ability, and the Bible says we are to use whatever gifts God has given us to serve others, which is what I try to do. When it comes to my gift, the result for the person I read for is a higher level of healing and/or a deeper faith in God and heaven. If the devil is posing as these spirits who are bringing so much peace and joy to the people I read for, then he really sucks at his job.

Are there evil spirits beyond this world? Yes, but I avoid them if I feel them and their negative energy coming through. They very rarely approach me, but when one does, I know it instantly. Is it possible that the devil is disguised as the spirits who come through to me? Again — yes, but because of my awareness of and sensitivity to that possibility, I won't let the devil in. For example, I recall a time when I gave a reading to someone and I felt a negative spirit coming through that made me feel physically ill. I immediately stopped what I was doing to get away from that spirit. Everything I do in my readings is based on feelings and signs. I connect with only those spirits who are in a good light, those who come through in a peaceful manner and with positive energy, those I know are in a good and healthy place. If I receive one that does not feel right, I stop the reading, energetically disconnect from the evil spirit, and call upon archangels (through meditation) for protection until I know that spirit is gone. My decision to disconnect from them is no different than the choice anyone has between good and evil in other situations. If you know something isn't right, or doesn't feel right, your instincts tell you not to do it. So don't do it. If you choose to do it anyway, then you have consciously chosen to let the devil in.

This is why I believe that what I have is a gift and not some- thing people should try to do just because they want to. You have to be very careful when you open yourself up to the other side. For example, I don't use a Ouija board, because it is a very real thing created by humans. I tried it in my early days when first discovering this gift; but I realized it wasn't for me, because it was an open door to evil. The darker energies can trick you into believing that what you are hearing is from a loved one, when it is not. When I use my gift, the messages I convey are based on love, or I simply do not convey them. Sure, I could let those dark spirits in and tell you that your Aunt Betty is coming through, that she hates you, and that she says you are going to rot in hell. But I never even come close to reaching that point. That's the difference between me and someone who uses a gift such as this for something sinister.

I am not going to generally defend those who call themselves mediums and psychics. There are too many phonies out there, and there are some who definitely will let the evil side in. There is a fine line there, and people have to be careful. But I use the gift God gave me with his will in mind. A reading with me is a beautiful experience and leads people to hope. I believe when we are given a gift by God, no matter what it is, we can choose to be Leonardo da Vinci or we can draw stick figures instead. In other words, we can use it to its fullest goodness and create something beautiful with it, or we can be lazy and let it go to waste. I have chosen the former with my gift. I use it with integrity and love and fulfill its most extreme potential. And I always will.

I understand why Grandma and others think the way they do. Heck, it took me years to come to terms with and accept this ability even though I was experiencing it every day. I just want to assure people that the spirits who communicate with me — the ones I bring through to you — are in heaven. They are good spirits with good intentions who want nothing more than to bring goodness to us.

As I have matured and have continued to develop this gift, my faith has actually grown stronger. My relationship with God has become more personal, as I think happens with all of us raised with faith, as we age. I have learned how to pray to him, and I realize that the blessings I have received in life far outweigh the difficulties. I am blessed to have been chosen to receive such an incredible gift. In turn, I feel an obligation to share it with others, and I intend to do so until my time here on earth is done.

Grandma was instrumental in raising me, and I have the utmost respect and love for her. I always will, and she knows that. And while I'm certain she prays for me more than she prays for anybody else — because of her feelings about the work I do — I'm good with that. In fact, I appreciate having someone love me as much as she does.

But like others who have any religious or spiritual vocation, I simply cannot ignore my calling. It would be a gift from God wasted if I did.

The Bottom Box

There were about twenty boxes full of miscellaneous items stacked in two rows in my garage that I hadn't unpacked since we'd moved into our home. I was going through them one day looking for something in particular, but with no luck. After opening nearly every one, I gave up.

A few days after that, I met Bill at a restaurant for dinner. It wasn't for a reading. I had known Bill for years, and we were very close friends. When I did have readings with him, though, they were always enlightening. I enjoyed them so much, and Bill always knew that anytime he felt any messages for me through his psychic or medium abilities, even outside of a formal reading, he had a free pass to tell me.

"Your grandma is coming through to me," he said during our dinner. "She's showing me a bear with red hearts and a note for you. She says it's in your garage, in a box in the corner, at the bottom of some other boxes."

The note and bear meant nothing to me. Those weren't the items I had been looking for a few days earlier. In fact, I was the one who had packed the boxes when we moved, and I didn't remember seeing a note or bear. But when I went back home, knowing Bill's track record for being right, I checked. Sure enough, there was a box on the very bottom of one of the stacks I hadn't looked in. I moved all the other boxes off it and opened it up. I dug through — and there they were.

A small, white, plush bear speckled with red hearts, along with a handwritten note addressed to me. It was from my grandma's best friend, JoAnn.

Dear Jessica,

Hope this scripture will be of comfort to you.

"But just as it is written, things which eye has not seen and ear has not heard,

And which have not entered the heart of man,

All that God has prepared for those who love him."

1 Corinthians 2:9

I know the love between a grandmother and granddaughter is very, very special. And that love will go on forever in your heart.

Love,

JoAnn

I broke down right there in the garage and cried like a baby. My grandma raised me. We were best friends. To say we were close does not do our relationship justice. When I had lost her, about five years earlier, in 2004, a part of me died, too. I had many difficult days over several years while trying to cope with her death.

But the bear and note brought a part of me back to life as I recalled the unbreakable bond and countless happy times we had together. When I thought back to Grandma's funeral, I vaguely remembered JoAnn giving me the bear and note, but I had completely forgotten about both because I was in a state of shock and was grieving at the time.

To find them again in the garage was absolutely the greatest gift I had ever received, one of those beautiful blessings in life that you never expect to happen. I keep the bear and that scripture on my desk at home where I see them every day, which makes me think of Grandma. I still miss her so much, but I have tremendous peace inside me now – a sense of closure – that I didn't have before.

Jessica

PART II

How It Works

Chapter 8

PSYCHICS versus MEDIUMS

Trust that you are here for a bigger purpose. Let your gift of light shine and guide you to where you need to be.

There are psychics, there are mediums, and there are psychic mediums. I am a psychic medium, though the work I do is usually that of a medium. All mediums are psychics, because they have that intuitive quality; but not all psychics are mediums, because they do not communicate with the deceased. You have to be a psychic to be a medium because, as a medium, you need to use your psychic senses to connect with and channel the spirits.

Confusing? Though this may not be an ideal, apples-to-apples comparison, look at it in terms of math teachers. There are individuals who know math, those who can teach math, and those who are math teachers. All those who can teach math know math, but not all of those who know math can teach it.

The difference in how I utilize my psychic abilities separately from my medium abilities is also a bit tricky to explain. As a psychic, I am "tuning in" to the energy of the spiritual side. As a medium, I am "channeling" that spiritual energy and letting the information I receive flow through my psychic senses. Picture a radio. I turn the dial and encounter a lot of static until I find a clear station. That is the tuning in, or the psychic side. Listening to and processing the information emitted from that station so that I can disseminate it to others is the "channeling," or medium side.

Psychics can tune into the past, present, and future and can make predictions by aligning the energy of the living with energy from the spiritual side. An example occurred in the class at the metaphysical shop, when I held the woman's ring and then read for her and described her home. I did it by using the energy from the ring and aligning it with my spiritual energy, which I collected when I closed my eyes and essentially performed short bursts of meditation.

One way I kept the psychic portion of my gift sharp during my college years was by predicting who would come down the hallway next or what they would be wearing. Sometimes I was wrong. Most of the time I was right. Some may call it a guessing game, but I was not randomly guessing. It was based on my intuition — that gut feeling that emerges when I tap into my spiritual side.

I think we can all groom ourselves to be psychic to a small extent because we are all spiritual beings before we are human beings. We are spirits occupying human bodies. If you've ever been to a visitation for someone who has died, you know what I mean. The body is nothing more than a shell that remains behind in death. The spirit — the soul — that once brought life to that person is what has departed. I believe that when we are alive in those shells, and we align our physical side with our spiritual side — our true nature — we can tap deeper into our intuition.

If you've seen the movie *Ghost*, you may recall the subway scene in which Patrick Swayze's character, who had died earlier in the film, was trying to move the bottle cap along the ground with his finger but couldn't do it. Every time he tried to push it, his finger went right through it. The other guy in the scene, played by Vincent Schiavelli, who was also dead but who knew from experience how to move the cap, told Patrick that the reason he was unable to move the cap was because he was too focused on the physical.

"You want to move something? You got to move it with your mind. You got to focus," Vincent told him. Patrick asked him how to focus.

"I don't know how you focus, you just focus!" Vincent said as he flicked the cap across the ground. "You got to take all your emotions...and push it way down here into the pit of your stomach, and then let it explode like a reactor!"

That scene was a good example of one of the simplest ways I know to create that physical and spiritual alignment. The "how" is definitely difficult to explain. I know it's just a movie, but he's right — I don't know how you focus, you just focus.

A medium differs from a psychic in that a medium is in direct communication with the spirit world — with specific spirits who once roamed the earth as human beings. They were once in physical bodies, but now they connect with a medium by channeling information to him so that he can share that information with the living.

All spirits can connect with me — good, bad, and every one in between. I spoke earlier about occasions when evil spirits have tried to get through. I believe that spirits are on different levels on the other side. Angels are at the highest level because they have never been in physical bodies on earth. They are the purest form of love. Those of us on earth who cross over will enter the other side at various levels but can ascend to higher levels as our souls continue to learn and grow.

For example, if someone who led a very good life dies at the same time as a man who once committed a heinous crime, the two of them likely would not enter the other side at the same level. The criminal could eventually ascend to a higher level, but it would take him time to do that as he paid his debts for his actions on earth. I once did a reading for a woman whose former brother-in-law, who had molested her niece and nephew, came through. She had been very happy when he died — that's how much she hated him, and he knew how much she hated him. So she was shocked when, during the reading, he wanted to speak to her. He wanted me to convey to her that he was sorry for what he had done and for all of the lives he had ruined. My take on that encounter is that once he got to the other side, he was able to clearly see how horrific his actions were, something he had refused to acknowledge when he was in the flesh. Once he crossed over, all his baggage — fear, sadness, depression, hatred, and so on — was released, enabling him to see his earthly actions in a different light. He then had the option to continue learning while over there. If he chose not to, he would stay at that lower level or even descend.

I told you the story about Kimberly's son, Michael, who took his own life. So yes, even those who commit suicide can communicate with me, but they start at very low levels. I believe every person has a soul contract before he is born. The terms include who his family is going to be, the everyday people he will encounter (his soul group), the lessons he will learn for

himself and that he will teach others while on earth, and his exit
point. But he can choose to breach that contract and exit his life
on earth early — a misguided and spiritually destructive choice.
Through suicide, he not only abandons the lessons he signed up
for, but he also abandons his soul group and the lessons he was
meant to teach them as part of *their* soul contracts. He may have
released himself from his physical body, but he cannot escape the
emotional pain, especially without the numbing effect of earthly
distractions — money, sex, drugs, food, and so on. A bodiless
soul is left only with the emotional state, which is, ironically, the
one thing the soul tried to escape on earth.

As a medium, I connect often with souls who have crossed
over after taking their own lives. Their commonly shared senti-
ment is regret for the pain they caused their families and loved
ones. I've also witnessed the gamut of emotions of those close to
them who were left behind here. All the lessons for everybody
involved — here and on the other side — center on love and
forgiveness and, ultimately, peace.

I believe everybody can receive signs from the other side. As
I will discuss, you already likely receive more signs than you
know. You don't recognize them because, instead of seeing the
events that unfold around you as signs from spirits, you see them
as coincidences, or you don't recognize them at all because you
have not tapped into that possibility — you have not aligned
your physical side with your spiritual side.

But even though everybody can receive and recognize signs,
not everybody can connect directly with the spirits and receive
specific information the spirits are trying to send. In fact, very

few people can. Grandpa may send you a sign by causing a light-bulb in your kitchen to suddenly burn out. It's possible he did it just to let you know he is there, but there may be more that he wants to communicate to you. You also do not know for sure that it is him, because you have not received any clear validation that it is. Not everybody can be a messenger like I am. That is where my gift comes into play.

Someone once told me that she wanted to communicate with the dead and had tried to do it by meditating and telling someone she knew who had died to show himself to her. I told her that probably wasn't going to happen, no matter how hard she tried. Spirits who have crossed over don't normally work that way, because, in my opinion, they don't want to scare the crap out of us. There are rare exceptions when they do appear, of course, such as when my mom appeared to me. But that was something she did on her own and for her own reasons; it was not something I had asked for. And although I continued to sleep in that room in the days after she appeared, hoping that she would return, she did not. When a spirit has me relay a message to a person, it's normally a pretty emotional moment for that person. Imagine if I were able to make that spirit visibly appear. I'd have to have a full-time psychologist on staff just to handle the aftereffects of my readings. That's why spirits send signs instead — such as maybe leaving something of personal significance in your pocket — to let you know they are there.

Having the gift of being a psychic medium is, in many re-spects, like having any other gift. I am sure that musically most people can hold a single note if they really try. However, that does not mean everybody sings like Pavarotti. Most people can shoot a basketball into a basket, but it does not mean everybody has the talent that LeBron James has. If someone is physically

built like LeBron, works as hard at getting better at basketball as
he does, and has the same passion for the game that he does, but
does not come anywhere close to his talent level, why is that?
The only answer is that LeBron was born with an uncommon
gift.

The biggest misunderstanding about psychic mediums is that
we know everything, or should know everything. Trust me, I've
heard all the jokes. "Why do I need to make an appointment
with you? You should already know I'm coming!" Haha! Yes, I
get that one, or jokes in the same vein, all the time. They're old,
but I roll with them.

Here are three things everybody should keep in mind regarding psychic mediums:

1. We are psychic mediums, not God.
2. God does not want us to know everything.
3. Your free will can always trump anything we say.

Some people think it would be cool to know everything before it happens. I think that would be devastating to the human
race. I don't see how we would be able to psychologically func-
tion if we knew everything that was going to happen before it
happened. We would all be worried about what we know is
going to occur tomorrow or, even worse, how we are going
to try to alter what we know is going to happen. Chaos would
ensue. What would be the point of human existence if we knew
everything? There would be little or no joy in anything. There
would be no spontaneity in our lives. Nothing in life would be a
journey if we knew the end before we started.

Psychic mediums also cannot know everything all the time
because we cannot tap into our spiritual side all day and every

day. I mentioned earlier that spirits reside at a very high level. They have to come down to me, and I have to go up to them, so we can meet somewhere in between and I can receive their messages. It's an exhausting process. They cannot stay down at that level, and I cannot stay up at that level, without having to recharge at some point. It's like being underwater. I can hold my breath for only so long before I need air to reenergize. Take an Olympic-gold-medal swimmer, for example. She worked hard to be the best in the world, but I bet she would also agree that she was born with a gift that helped her accomplish what she accomplished. Even with that gift, though, she cannot swim all the time. What would happen if she tried to swim twenty-four hours a day, seven days a week? She'd eventually become a spirit. She couldn't physically survive! Nobody can be tuned into his or her gift all the time, no matter what it is.

And then there is free will. Yes, I can make a prediction about something that will happen to you. In fact, my intuition could be so strong that I could almost guarantee something is going to happen. But that word "almost" always has to be included, because God created us so that we can think for ourselves and make our own decisions. If I tell you that you are going to take a trip to Mexico next month, and your friend calls you the next day and asks if you want to go to Mexico next month, I cannot prevent you from declining the offer if you choose to. You can change the outcome of what I predicted. Of course, then I'd be asked, "Well then, why didn't you know I would be asked to go but would decline the invitation?" Again, free will from God. I do not have control over or insight into the world's 7 billion brains. That is why I always tell people to use me as a guide, not as a be-all and end-all. You are in charge of your life. I can, with the intervention of spirits, offer insight to help you improve your life, but I cannot control it.

Another important thing to note about psychics and mediums is that very few are truly either one. Out of the 7 billion people on the planet, maybe just a few thousand, if that, can legitimately claim to be psychics or mediums. What can be difficult to do, yet which is obviously extremely important, is to distinguish between the legitimate ones and the scammers, those generally in it for money.

One sign of scam artists is when they tell you that you have a dark cloud enveloping you and the only way to remove it, or to jar your karma back into place, is to give them money. Another sign is when they are primarily negative in their so-called reading or are consistently vague in what they tell you. They are playing with your emotions and want nothing more than your money. All psychics and mediums will share vague insights — not everything they share will be as specific as the color and design of your underwear. But if they stay vague and their reading doesn't build toward specifics that are impossible for just anyone to know, be careful.

I recently went to a palm reader on the streets of New York City to see what she would come up with. It took her less than a minute to determine that I was in danger and should fork over some more green so that she would be able to see and reveal that danger. I told her I knew what she was doing and that she should stop because it was not right. She was flabbergasted by my gall and shooed me away. I'm sure she got her money from the next person, but it felt good to call her on it.

On that same trip, I stopped at another psychic shop with my friend Michelle, the one who had led me to Dakota. The psychic, without any prompting from us (we hadn't said anything other than hello), put her hand on Michelle's belly and told her that she should stop stressing about getting pregnant, that it would eventually happen, and that she would have a boy and a girl. That comment, especially since it was her first one and she uttered it the split second we walked in, was fascinating. Michelle had been trying unsuccessfully to get pregnant for years, and it had been weighing heavily on her mind. What that psychic did not know was that I had given Michelle an identical reading, with precisely the same details, just a few weeks earlier. I could tell that this psychic was legit, not just because of her prediction about the pregnancy but because of the compassion she showed, several other pieces of specific and factual information she shared about Michelle throughout the reading, and the fact that she did not ask for more money.

When it comes to my readings, or any reading from a legitimate psychic medium, you must realize there is rarely anything exact about them. It's not a black-and-white business. My purpose in connecting a spirit with someone is to relay the signs and messages I receive; but the form in which I receive them varies, and how I interpret them is a fluid process. Be skeptical as you receive a reading, if you'd like. In fact, I encourage it in order to help you weed out the fakes. But also leave your mind open to the many possibilities that could come your way from those of us who are genuine.

I Would Give My Life . . .

About two months after my husband, John, died, I went to one of Bill's shows on a whim with my friend Joy. I wouldn't say I was an atheist, but my husband and son were. And I had read enough about mediums to know every trick in the book. I wanted to witness firsthand how mediums manipulate people.

According to all the books I'd read, the "medium" is supposed to ask twenty, rapid-fire questions before he gets a hit, and then zero in on that information, creating the illusion of clairvoyance. But Bill wasn't doing that.

I knew one of the bouncers working at the theater, so I slipped into the back of the room to find out what was going on. "I don't get it," I whispered. "How is he doing this? Are you people feeding him our credit card information?"

He laughed and said, "We would never do that!"

"Then does he plant actors in the audience?"

"No, no," he said convincingly. "He's the real deal."

After the show, my mind went over and over what we had witnessed. How did he do it? I tried desperately to see the show through the familiar tricks outlined in a book I had read, but none of them applied. Nothing explained what I'd witnessed.

What I didn't know then was that I had been set before Bill Philipps in preparation for losing Jonpaul, our son. At age twenty-three, Jonpaul died eleven months after his father, succumbing to an antibiotic-resistant infection (MRSA). He was, like his father, an extraordinary individual: kind to the core, thoughtful, and the smartest person in the room. John and Jonpaul, the two brightest lights in my life, gone.

But Bill would present to me the idea that they were not really gone, that we live in the material world and the spiritual realm interacts with our world in meaningful ways. Soon after Jonpaul died, I called and made an appointment with Bill. I provided a fake email address and a fake name and paid with a money order.

Two days before the appointed time, I visited Jonpaul's Facebook page and posted this message: "I would give my life to throw my arms around you one last time." Then I noticed something strange. My daughter, Jaime, had posted our favorite picture of Jonpaul. In it, he was three years old and wearing his sister's baseball mitt. The Facebook picture was different from the original. There was a bright light surrounding him, shooting out from his form. I didn't understand how it got there. But I would after meeting with Bill at his office.

"Hi, JJ," Bill said.

"Hello!" I said, smiling but nervous.

"Now JJ isn't your real name, is it?" he asked.

"No, it's not." A good guess, I thought. "It's Jennifer."

"Okay, Jennifer. Right off, I am getting three men. All three are *J*s. You have a lot of *J*s around you!"

In fact, we do, but I did not offer this information.

"First. An older man. He passed maybe twenty years ago. He's above you, meaning a father? Yes, your father…Did your father pass?"

I nodded.

"J…James, was his name James?"

I nodded, but James is probably the second-most popular male name beginning with a *J*, after John.

"And he passed twenty years ago or so?"

"Twenty-three years ago," I said.

Bill nodded distantly, as if he was listening to something I couldn't hear. "He had heart trouble. He's showing me his chest."

This was one of the common tricks. Most likely cause of death: heart disease or cancer. But it also happened to be true.

"He's showing me a shovel, and gold, something with a shovel and gold, like gold mining?" He seemed confused by this. "Does that mean anything to you?"

This gave me pause. "My dad's favorite vacation was panning for gold; we often went panning for gold." I was thinking that was a pretty darn good coincidence.

"He's telling me he is with a woman. She is on your mother's side? Older, maybe a grandmother? Her name starts with an M...M-E-R...Do you know who this is?"

"My mom's mom, my grandmother, was named Merle." My thoughts were spinning crazily. "But Dad wouldn't be with her. He never even liked my grandma."

"Jennifer," Bill chuckled, as if I were a very young child. "It is not like that there. There's no animosity, no dislikes. Besides, they were both gamblers, right?"

That was an excellent guess! My grandmother, like my dad, was a pretty serious gambler.

Bill quickly switched gears. "I'm getting the other two. It is kind of confusing, separating them. I'm getting a John. He is older. He's...is he your husband?"

"Yes."

"He died...he is showing me April 10th."

My heart leapt to greet this auspicious date. Adrenaline shot through my body, and as if preparing for danger, all senses went on high alert. "He died on April 10th," I said.

"He loves you. Oh, yes, lady," Bill laughed. "You are surrounded by his love."

Tears welled in my eyes; I was beginning to feel overwhelmed, but I realized I was waiting for Jonpaul. Almost impatiently, I was emotionally on the edge of my seat.

"I'm getting something...I'm a little confused." Bill let out a huge sigh before pausing for a long minute. "The other one is younger, much younger."

A hand covered my mouth; I couldn't speak.

"He's younger. A John too? No, like John but different..."

His name burst out of me. "Jonpaul!"

"Oh...Jonpaul. He is young. He died recently. I'm getting March 11th. This year? Does that mean anything to you?"

"Yes," I said in an emotion-laden whisper.

"Who is he to you? Is he family?"

"My son. Our son. John's and mine."

"Oh, I am so sorry…Okay, okay, now I get it. That's what's going on. They are together. John and Jonpaul."

I couldn't see through my tears. The idea that Jonpaul was there, with John – they were together. My heart couldn't bear it. I was afraid of the emotions surging through me; it was like waking from a nightmare to find yourself in an unexpected landscape, one where you are safe.

"Jonpaul wants you to know he is happy, very, very happy. He loves you so much. He's showing me how he died. Something to do with blood. His blood…an infection? Did he have a blood infection?"

"MRSA," I say.

"Okay, he loves you. Wow. You are very close."

I was participating in a miracle.

"Jonpaul is coming in loud…He is telling me that something happened yesterday or the day before, I can't tell which. You were looking at your computer…his Facebook page? It was pretty intense."

I managed to tell him what happened.

Bill nodded. "He was with you.

"They're telling me there is someone else…a female. Another J name. My God, there are *a lot* of Js around you! Do you have a daughter?"

"Yes. Jaime, our daughter, Jonpaul's sister."

"They're showing me September 9th. Does that mean anything to you?"

"It's Jaime's birthday."

"Also, does she surf? Jonpaul is showing me her on a board in the ocean? What does that mean?"

"She does surf, but she paddleboards all the time. It's her favorite thing."

"Yes, he is with her when she does this. He is watching over her, keeping her safe."

I hold up my hand to stop.

"You don't need me, Jennifer," he said. "You three are very close; you're very connected. They are surrounding you with their love. Jennifer, you don't know how lucky you are."

My world had just changed and I knew, even in that moment, that it was not going to be a small change. I was unable to speak; my brain felt on fire, as if fueled by high-octane information.

Still crying, hands over my heart, I finally got up to leave. "Bill," I confess, "you don't know how hard this was. You don't know John and Jonpaul. They were hard-core empiricists, atheists."

"Not anymore, they're not," he said with a smile.

I laughed through my tears; it was the funniest line I'd ever heard.

"Jennifer, may I hug you?"

I nodded, but something else slipped into my awareness. Bill was almost as tall as Jonpaul. He had the same broad shoulders. He did not seem that much older. I stepped into Bill's embrace. His arms came around me. I felt his love, but just for a second, before it became something much more, an answer to my most fervent wish: *I would give my life to throw my arms around you one last time...*

I could not let go.

Jennifer

Chapter 9

MEDITATION

Learning to trust your intuition takes time. The only way to accomplish this is through meditation – by silencing the mind and listening inward.

I f you have meditated before, especially on a regular basis, you know how much the practice can improve your mental fortitude. As a medium, I recognize that it is absolutely critical for me to have a clear and open mind in order to give effective readings. That's why I do a deep meditation each morning and a brief meditation before each reading.

Meditation is an essential behind-the-scenes exercise that few clients know I do. And why would they even care? When they come to me for a reading, they want one thing: for me to connect them with spirits by whatever means necessary. That's it. They couldn't care less what I do before they arrive. But the fact is that if I don't properly prepare before their readings, the countless earthly distractions in my personal life that continually infiltrate my mind could interfere with the spirits' attempts to communicate with me and, ultimately, with my clients.

Meditation is to the mind of a medium what warming up is to the body of an athlete. Few athletes would say they "enjoy" warming up. They probably don't mind it — it makes them feel good and ready to go — but it does take time and effort, and there is nothing glamorous about it. Fans want to know how their favorite player scored that winning touchdown, swam in record time, or hit the game-winning basket, not how well his or her muscles were loosened up in the locker room before the game. But all athletes know they cannot just roll out of bed in the morning, go straight to their competition, and expect to be successful. If they don't warm up first, they could cramp up, lose focus in their mission, and be unable to perform at their highest level.

Something comparable can happen to my mind before a reading. If I don't meditate, my mind could cramp up with all kinds of useless information that doesn't pertain to the reading at hand. That could cause me to lose focus during the reading and hinder me from connecting with the spirits as clearly as I should, for the sake of the spirits and my client.

The primary reason why I *need* to meditate and clear my mind of junk is because of the fine line between my own thoughts (the left side of my brain, or analytical side) and the presence of spirits (the right side of my brain, or intuitive side).

Let's say I have a reading to give one afternoon, and then later that night I'm throwing a thirtieth birthday party at my house for my friend Tyler. During the reading, I happen to see images of music, crowds of people, food, drinks, the number thirty, or someone named Tyler. It seems obvious that my consciousness has created a visualization of the party I am going to throw. But is that really what's happening? What if a spirit coming through during the reading is named Tyler, or used to be a musician who played in front of big crowds, or is someone who worked in a restaurant or died when he was in his thirties? You can see that fine line.

So how do I tell where those images are coming from? That's where meditation comes into play.

If I clear my mind through meditation, any images created by my own consciousness after that will generally be presented in a story pattern. If I am thinking about the party, it will have a flow to it, like reading a story or watching a short movie clip: first the guests will arrive, then Tyler will arrive, then I'll turn the music on, then we will eat. If those images are being put in my mind by a spirit, they are usually conveyed very quickly, like flash cards. I may see pictures of all those things I mentioned a moment ago, but in no particular order or context.

If I do not meditate, I may have a more difficult time figuring out where those images are coming from. If I'm stressed-out about the party and do not meditate before the reading, my consciousness may cause those images — the music, crowds of people, food, drinks, and so on — to flash rather than flow because of my anxiety level, making it difficult for me to tell whether it's the spirit or me putting those images in my head.

My meditation process is very simple. I do it each morning for fifteen to thirty minutes on average and then again very briefly before each reading.

For the morning meditation, I sit in a chair in a quiet room with all electronic gadgets turned off. I close my eyes and put my hands on my lap, palms facing up. I breathe slowly and deeply, concentrating on feeling and listening to each breath. I mentally surround myself with white light, which I regard as a representation of God and everything that is peaceful. If this sounds like what I did in the haunted house, it's because it's exactly what I did. The only difference is that in a general meditation, I'm not trying to guide anxious spirits to that light. All I'm trying to do is achieve a sense of tranquility that is difficult to attain without escaping the type of minute-to-minute interruptions we all encounter each day.

As I sit there in silence with the white light around me, I ask God to help me provide my clients that day with the best readings that I possibly can. I ask him to remove everything in my mind that is inconsequential to the readings, and to let the spirits know I am open to their presence — in other words, I'm open for business. What that does is transform me into a messenger for the spirits. My mind has been emptied and is ready for them to enter, with plenty of room for anything they want to tell me. Physically, it makes me feel lighter. My blood pressure drops and my body slows down, creating a somewhat light-headed sensation. That's when I know the meditation is working.

In November 2014, I did a show at the Belterra Casino in southern Indiana. After telling the audience about myself, I asked them to participate in a brief meditation with me — maybe five to seven minutes — to clear their minds and to welcome their deceased loved ones into their hearts. I guess you could call it a condensed version of my morning meditation. It wasn't anything I had prepared — it just came to me on stage. To watch a crowd of nearly one thousand people immerse themselves in this exercise was an awesome sight, and they really seemed to enjoy it. The following is how I did that meditation. You can use it for yourself (you can record yourself saying it and play it back when you need it), or use it as a guide to create your own personal meditation. It's most effective when read slowly in a dark and quiet setting. Soft background music might also be a nice touch.

Close your eyes.

Focus solely on your breath. Listen to yourself breathe.

Slowly inhale . . . exhale . . . inhale . . . exhale. Breathe in a circular pattern. Honor your body's continuous motion.

Feel more and more peace with each breath you take.

Now visualize yourself on the beach in the middle of paradise.

Feel the warmth of the sun . . . and the gentle breeze. Hear the soothing waves rolling onto the shore.

Feel the comfort of the soft sand between your toes.

Connect yourself with Mother Earth.

Release what no longer serves you well. Any disease. Any illness. Any negativity. Any people who bring you down. Any situations that cause stress. Just let them go. Release them into the universe. They are gone. They are no longer part of you.

Now see a brilliant white light spiraling down from heaven. Accept it. Feel its peace. Its love. Its warmth.

The light spirals around you and protects you from anything negative and unwanted.

It gently travels through your head. Through your throat. Through your shoulders. Into your chest.

Feel it pause there and deeply warm your heart.

Now it travels down your arms, through your hands, and into your fingertips.

The light goes back up your arms and then cascades down through your torso. Through your thighs. Through your calves. It covers every inch of your body and soul before exiting through your feet.

But the light does not leave you.

It anchors you securely to Mother Earth.

This beautiful, crystal-clear light is the light of God. It is your protector. Nothing negative can penetrate it. It is now part of you.

Now invite in your loved ones who have passed.

See them with your mind.

Feel them with your heart.

Welcome each one of them with peace and love. Smile at them. Embrace them. Share your love with them.

Always know that, no matter what situation you are in, they are just a thought away. Open your mind, open your heart, and you will feel them.

Continue to breathe. Slowly. In and out. Hear yourself breathe. In . . . out . . . in . . . out.

Feel the peace within you. Feel the love. Feel the warmth.

Feel the gentle light of God.

Now open your eyes.

The meditation I do by myself between individual readings is not as intense but is still very important. The length of time I spend doing it depends on a few factors, including how much time I have until the next reading begins and how stressful my previous reading was.

I try to schedule fifteen to thirty minutes between readings to give me enough time to wind down from my previous reading. Usually, though, I can do my meditation in a minute or two. That may not sound like much time to prepare, but look at it like a boxing match. Boxers will go all out during a round, then take a one-minute break before the next round. What's a minute? To those boxers, it's everything. They have conditioned themselves to make the most of those brief time-outs by resetting their minds and bodies and returning to the ring reenergized.

I may need more time if I have just finished providing someone with a reading that was chaotic, meaning many spirits came through and/or the client experienced a lot of emotion. In either case, I may take a few extra minutes to clear my mind. It's sort of like cleaning up a table in a restaurant after a group has left, in order to get that table ready for the next group. If the former party included rambunctious people who left behind a lot to be cleaned up, it will take a little longer to get the table set for the next party.

One thing I am careful not to do is meditate too long. If I meditate too long, it opens the door for too many spirits to come in too soon. This doesn't happen frequently, but it does happen. For example, if I have an 11 AM reading with Lisa and 1 PM reading with Angela, a spirit related to Angela could show up for Lisa's reading. Spirits are anxious — they want to reach their loved ones and will jump at every chance they have to get inside my head. If a spirit who is focused on Angela intrudes on Lisa's reading, it can throw everything into a state of flux. That is why I like to meditate in the morning, well before my readings start, then for just a minute or two before each reading. Meditation is good, but too much of a good thing can reduce its positive effects.

I doubt that all mediums follow the protocol I do when preparing for a reading, but the chances are pretty good that they meditate in some form. If I do a reading for you, don't be afraid to ask me if I meditated. The answer will always be yes, but just hearing me say that may help you open your mind more — knowing that I have opened mine for the spirits to reach you.

If you have never meditated, or you don't do so on a regular basis, I highly recommend that you do. No matter who you are or how busy your life is, squeeze in time for it. There are many ways to meditate. Just find what brings you calm and inner peace, and practice it daily. Some ways I meditate include listening to music, lighting candles, and burning frankincense. You may enjoy yoga, taking a walk, writing in a diary, or doing artwork. Even just leaving the radio off in the car on your way to work and enjoying the quiet can be a form of meditation.

Clear out the energy that is holding you down, and welcome the energy that will lift you up.

I Raised My Hand

My wife is very big on anything spiritual and positive, and she has always talked about Bill's inspirational posts on Facebook. When she found out Bill was coming to New York in 2014 for an audience reading, she absolutely had to be there.

Me? I went with her for the same reason that I had gone with her to see other mediums – to support her and to get out of the house for a night of entertainment. Aside from that, it didn't mean much to me. Do I believe that some mediums can do what they claim? Maybe. Am I skeptical? Without a doubt. My attitude is that if you throw everything at the wall, something is bound to stick.

Bill started his show with a meditation. He asked us to close our eyes, pay attention to our breathing, and envision ourselves in a peaceful place. I usually don't participate in that with other mediums, but I did this time; nothing wrong with giving your mind a little break. His meditation was very relaxing, and it certainly got me focused on the present moment.

When the meditation was finished, he came down from the stage and was reading for somebody in the audience near us. He was only about two minutes in when he stopped.

"I'm getting something from Steven," he said. "Who has a connection to a Steven?"

My wife's eyes lit up.

I kept my mouth shut.

"He's telling me he took his own life," Bill said. "Someone here knows him."

I was stunned. *No way*, I thought. But how could I fight two specific validations such as those? I couldn't. I slowly raised my hand and was the only one in the auditorium to do so. Steven was my brother.

Bill acknowledged me when he saw my hand go up, but then he got sidetracked by another spirit and started giving a reading to someone else. Now I didn't know what was going on.

Is he going to come over here? I thought. *How does this work? Did Steven leave?*

Nope, Steven didn't go anywhere. After Bill finished that other reading, he came right over to me and the floodgates opened. He gave me validation after validation letting me know that it was my brother, and that he was in a better place and very happy.

Steven told Bill that I should go ahead and fix up the bathroom, as I had been planning on doing for a couple of weeks. He told Bill that I should go to the stadium and "go see it." I knew the "it" he was referring to was a brick I bought at Citi Field, home of the New York Mets – my brother's favorite team. I had ordered it in his memory and had it engraved with his name, but I never took the time to go see it.

Bill talked about our grandmother by name and said Steven was with her.

One of the funny validations was Bill's mention of Super Mario Brothers. Who would come up with something like that? Just before Steven passed, he had given me his old Nintendo video game player. The only game he included with it was Super Mario Brothers.

Then there was the validation that really moved me: "He's talking about *The Wizard of Oz,*" Bill said. "He says he was just watching it with you."

My wife and I had taken a family vacation in the Bahamas the week before with our two little boys. One night in our hotel room, we watched *The Wizard of Oz,* which was not only one of Steven's favorite movies but also a movie that I remember watching with him several times when we were young.

Bill definitely had something going on that night. And when I say that, I don't mean that he was right 40 percent or 50 percent or 60 percent of the time. He was right with me 95 percent of the time.

It was an evening that shook me up, but in a good way. When you lose somebody close to you, it's a good feeling when they reach out. It definitely made me more of a believer, gave me some closure, and made me realize that even though Steven is gone it's okay for me to move on.

I know now that my brother is in a better place. And because of that, I am now in a better place.

Rich

Chapter 10

THEIR VOICES

The universe and spirits will help you manifest what you want, but you need to be open to their assistance.

use six types of spiritual senses to receive information:

- Clairvoyance — the ability to see beyond what the physical eye can see (with our "inner eye")
- Clairaudience — the ability to hear beyond what the physical ear can hear
- Clairsentience — the ability to feel a spirit (what people describe as a "gut feeling")
- Claircognizance — the ability to just know without using any of the other senses
- Clairgustance — the ability to taste beyond what the physical taste buds can taste
- Clairalience — the ability to smell beyond what the physical nose can smell

As information flows through the channel from a spirit to me, I receive it through one of the six "clairs." The clairs are intuitive correlations with our physical senses of sight, sound, touch, taste, and smell. The clairs go beyond the physical and into the psychical. I never literally see a spirit (at least I haven't since I saw my mom after she died) or hear a spirit's actual voice. The communication always happens through one of the clairs, which is why I need to be open to all of my senses during every reading.

One of the clairs most commonly used by psychic mediums is clairvoyance. The spirits insert messages into my mind using images of their choice. My consciousness then shows me those images, which I relay to the person I am reading for.

Some mediums call clairvoyance a "download" of information. When you download something onto your computer, there is normally a graphic that shows the pieces of the file being transferred. The percentage of completion quickly goes up until it hits 100 percent. That's how rapidly spirits can throw information at me. The reason they do it in that manner, I believe, is because they reside at such a high level of energy that they need to exert an exorbitant amount of power to come down to a level where I can receive information from them — and they cannot stay at that level for long. As I mentioned earlier, we all have to recharge at some point. So in the short amount of time they have, it's important for them to throw their messages at me as quickly and succinctly as possible.

Communicating with spirits through clairvoyance is very similar to playing a game of charades, which, if you have ever played the game, you know can be very frustrating. Unfortunately, a spirit doesn't always come right out and clearly say, "This is Tom. Please tell my daughter, Lynn, that I am at peace." Instead, Tom may identify himself by throwing his initials at me, or he may give me his middle name. If he has a sense of humor, he may show me a picture of actor Tom Cruise, or he may be even more vague by showing me a scene from one of Cruise's movies, which will leave me wondering what exactly he is trying to say about the movie. He could also try to validate who he is by telling me his birth date, but he might not make it easy and give me his birth date in numbers. If he was born around Christmas, he may flash me a fir tree or a picture of Santa Claus. All spirits are different, but their personalities on the other side are generally the same as they were here. If an individual was shy on earth, it may take extra effort for me to get information from her. If she had a giant sense of humor on earth, she will probably let that sense of humor shine when communicating with me, making our "game" a little more challenging for me.

Once I have a good idea that it is Tom trying to come through, he will begin to confirm his presence by sharing personal things about his daughter or special moments in life that the two of them shared and that nobody else would know about.

The spirits usually seem to realize that if they want success with me, they must communicate with me in a way I will understand. They have to use information from *my* memory bank — something I have already experienced or seen or learned in life and which will make sense to me. For example, I am not much of a sports guy. If a spirit has the same name as a well-known football player and is trying to convey his name to me by flashing a picture of that player or that player's team, I am not likely to get it, which could make for a frustrating reading.

I usually ask spirits to give me the simplest messages possible. If a spirit worked in construction during his life, I would want him to show me a hammer, not a big piece of heavy machinery that I may not recognize. If he was an accountant, a calculator or tax forms would be better than giving me the name of a specific accounting firm I've never heard of. If he was a writer, a book would be better than a photo of John Grisham — a well-known author, but someone I probably could not pick out of a lineup.

There are times, though, when specifics come in handy. Once as I did a reading for a young woman, a spirit showed me an image of the late actress Lucille Ball (known to her fans simply as "Lucy"). I had no idea what this spirit was trying to convey, but I did know who Lucy was, and I am confident the spirit knew that I would know. When I said "Lucille Ball" to the young woman, she smiled. People always said her mother looked like Lucy, so she knew it was her mother coming through to me. Had I not known who Lucy was, I probably would have tried to describe who I saw in general terms — a beautiful woman with red hair and a nice complexion. That might have led us to conclude that it was her mother, but it would not have been as definitive.

The point is that there are no rules in this game, and the spirits are the ones leading the reading. They will do whatever they think will get the attention of their loved ones and me, and whatever they think we will understand. They can be serious, funny, ornery. I once had a spirit named Eric make what appeared to be sarcastic statements to me that were addressed to the friend of his whom I was reading for. I hesitantly asked her if Eric was a sarcastic person, hoping not to offend her in any way. "You mean a total smartass?" she said. "Yep, that's my Eric!"

Clairvoyance is used by animals too. Yes, your pets are alive and well in the spirit world. This didn't really surprise me when I first realized it. If you've ever looked into the eyes of an animal, you know there's a soul in there. And a lot of people today, far more than in past generations, treat their pets as such. I've had readings in which someone's mother would come through and the client would say, "Yeah, okay...but are you getting anything from my dog?" We love our pets, they love us, and they let us know that from the other side.

No, they don't speak to me — sorry, your barking dog still can only bark. And they do not give us advice or direction in our lives like the spirits of humans give us. But they do put simple thoughts in my mind, such as a picture of themselves to let me know they are there. It's just their way of providing comfort to their owners who may be grieving their loss.

Many people would agree that most animals, especially pets, are creatures of pure and unconditional love — which is what I believe the spirit world is first and foremost about. It makes sense that the animals who once graced this earth would also be in a better place in the next life.

For me, clairaudience is as common as clairvoyance, and the two often go hand in hand. Clairaudience is the ability to hear beyond the capability of the human ear.

A perfect example of clairaudience and clairvoyance working together is when I was reading for my friend Rachel, the accountant. When Michael was coming through, trying to reach someone named Kimberly, I was seeing images (clairvoyance) such as a gun and a red pickup truck, but I was also hearing words (clairaudience) such as *Michael* and *Sacramento*. I wasn't hearing Michael's actual voice. I was hearing my voice, which was working as a messenger for Michael's voice. By using those two clairs, he was able to get his messages to me.

The most popular way spirits use clairaudience without clairvoyance is through music. Once, as a family came in for a reading, I had the song "Angel" by Sarah McLachlan playing in my head. I knew the song and knew it wasn't my own consciousness playing it, because it had been ages since I'd heard it. I told the family I was hearing it and, sure enough, their daughter who had recently died was named Angel.

One of my most significant readings involving clairaudience (and a little clairvoyance) was with a young man named Mark. His best friend had just passed away and now came through swiftly and clearly during our reading. Throughout the reading I kept hearing the song "Stairway to Heaven" by Led Zeppelin. Again, it was a song I had not heard in a long time, so I knew it was his friend playing it for me. "Does that song have any significance to you?" I asked Mark.

He smiled. "Yeah, that was his favorite song," Mark said. "They even played it at his service."

"He wants me to tell you that he is in a good place, and that you don't need to worry about him," I said. "He says anytime you hear this song, know that he is the one responsible for it being played."

Mark was beaming with happiness. I could have stopped there, but I was getting another message from his friend. "He is also showing me a white truck with the driver's window not working. Does that mean anything to you?"

"I own a white truck," Mark said. "In fact, I drove it here. But the window works, as far as I know."

After our reading was over, Mark left. He had just pulled out of the driveway when my phone rang. It was him. I couldn't tell whether he was laughing or crying...probably both.

"Bill?" he said. "Do you hear that?" In the background I could hear "Stairway to Heaven" playing on the radio. "And guess what?" he continued. "My freaking window won't go down!"

I can't say that even I expected Mark to hear the song that quickly, or for him to walk outside and find his window didn't work. But like I've said, spirits work in mysterious ways. You never know what they will do or when they will do it.

Clairsentience, the ability to feel a spirit, technically occurs in every reading that I give, because I always feel the presence of spirits as they come in, maybe through chills or a sudden warmth. But the term is more specifically used by mediums to describe spirits spontaneously impressing their feelings into the medium's feelings, generally in a way that shows how the departed person died. It is a spur-of-the-moment gut feeling. For example, I may get a heavy sensation in my lungs to validate that a person died of lung cancer. Or I may feel pressure on my chest, signifying that a person died of a heart attack. One of the best examples of clairsentience is the story I told earlier about Melissa and the train. I felt a spirit hit me so hard that it made me instinctively say that I felt as if I had been hit by a train. Imagine the spirit's joy when I blurted that out. I could have said I felt as if I'd just been hit by a ton of bricks, or by a car. But the spirit who came through did what she felt she needed to do to get me to say what she wanted me to say, and it worked!

Claircognizance is, to me, the most fascinating of the clairs because even I'm a bit befuddled about how it works and why the spirits don't use it more often. Claircognizance is simply just knowing something. It's suddenly — boom! A fact intended for the person I'm reading for pops into my head, and I know without a doubt it's true. The fact comes from a spirit, of course, but it's not like clairvoyance or clairaudience. It simply happens, in an instant.

A good example is a reading I once did for a private group. I was telling one of the women in the group that I felt her mother coming through. She smiled. Then I blindsided her. And the only reason I blindsided her was because I was blindsided by her mother communicating with me through claircognizance. "You're going through a divorce now, right?" I said.

Her smile vanished. "No!" she snapped. She looked shaken. But I knew I was correct. I moved on to other messages her mother was giving me, afraid to push the divorce issue, given her reaction, especially in front of her friends. A little while later, when we were taking a break, she pulled me aside and told me she had just filed for divorce from her husband. Nobody in the group with us knew about it, nor was she ready for them to know. I appreciated her telling me the truth — but even if she hadn't told me, I knew it was true. That is how convincing claircognizance is. And it is probably the easiest of the clairs for me to work with, because there are no games I have to play with the spirits to figure out what they are trying to tell me. It's nice when they afford me that luxury.

Clairgustance, the ability to taste, and clairalience, the ability to smell, usually occur simultaneously in my readings and often involve food. One example is an instance when I read for an older woman whose husband had passed away. The reading had gone well and I thought we were about finished, when I suddenly tasted and smelled Mexican food. The taste, I thought, was specifically enchiladas. Now most people don't cry when I talk about enchiladas, but it was understandable why she did.

She said, through her tears, not only that they were her husband's favorite meal but also that she had made them the previous weekend for herself in his memory.

These two clairs may come through to me less often than the other four, but they are extremely significant when they do. In my opinion, the spirits aren't able to eat or drink as spirits — they have no reason to — but they probably miss the physical sensation of enjoying a good meal, both its taste and its aroma. Let's face it, when you enjoy eating two or three meals a day for decades, you're likely going to miss it, no matter how good your new life is on the other side. So through clairgustance and clairalience, that woman's husband was able to both connect to his wife and share in and savor the experience of that meal with her the only way he knew how.

I have asked myself, especially in my early years of discovering this gift, why the spirits and I need all these clairs to communicate. Why do they show me only flashes of what they want to say? Why do I have to smell food to receive messages from them? Can you imagine how easy it would be for my clients and me if a spirit would just say, "Bill, please tell her..."? But it's not that easy, and I've accepted that. Once I get to the other side myself, I'll figure out why they do it the way they do. Until then, I'll keep doing what I do, as long as it effectively gets the spirits' messages to their loved ones.

My Two Sons in Heaven

I had a reading with Bill in the summer of 2014, hoping to connect with my grandfather, who died of cancer in 1999. We were very close, but I felt like I never got to say good-bye. I was pregnant when he died, and it is taboo in our Asian culture to attend a funeral if you are pregnant, because of the bad luck it could bring. I was upset that I couldn't go, but I did not want to offend anyone. I felt meeting with Bill could provide me with some closure.

Though he lived in the United States for much of his later life, my grandpa was born and raised in China. My concern was that Bill would not understand him, because Grandpa spoke only Chinese and Vietnamese. Bill assured me it would not be a problem, because spirits communicated most often with imagery. It would be Grandpa's job to communicate with Bill in a way that Bill would understand.

And Grandpa did just that. Bill gave me several validations that Grandpa was with us. Six in particular stood out: the final one was stunning, and it's still difficult today to put the emotions I felt into words.

The first validation was quick to come through. Bill asked me if Grandpa was a world traveler. I told him he wasn't. "But I'm seeing a globe in his hand," Bill said.

We were two minutes into the reading and I was already crying. When I was little, maybe nine years old, Grandpa took me to the Smithsonian in Washington, D.C., where they had an old wooden globe on display. Grandpa, not familiar with the importance or value of the artifact, started knocking on it just to make noise. He thought it was funny. Security did not. Fortunately, they didn't kick us out. It was one of those childhood memories that always stuck with me, and Grandpa knew it.

Bill then asked if I had remodeled my kitchen recently, because Grandpa was telling him that he liked it. I laughed. I had just remodeled it a few weeks earlier, and wondered who would specifically ask about a kitchen remodeling unless they knew me.

Then a name came through. "I'm seeing Austin…or Dustin… or Justin…or something similar," Bill said. My oldest son's name is Austin – he's the one I was pregnant with when Grandpa died. In Grandpa's honor, I made Austin's middle name the same as my grandpa's middle name. I couldn't have named my son after a more special person, and I was so happy that my grandpa knew who his great-grandson was.

The fourth validation, and one of the most intriguing to me, was when Bill was trying to give me another name. He struggled with it, for obvious reasons. The name was Dung (pronounced *Young*), an Asian name that Bill was unfamiliar with. Dung was one of my uncles – one of my grandpa's sons – who had many struggles in life and, in fact, is still homeless today. I knew it was a validation because of the message Grandpa had for Dung – "Let him know that he is a very important person despite his circumstances, and that I do hear him when he talks to me."

Bill continued to amaze me when he said that Grandpa wanted to know if I had been finding coins everywhere. I burst out laughing. I had just told my husband a few days earlier that our two-year-old son had been picking up so many coins lately – in restaurants, in stores, on the sidewalk, around the house – that I was going to have to start carrying a piggy bank everywhere we went.

Five stories – five validations. Then came the sixth, as the reading was winding down. "He is with your two sons," Bill said matter-of-factly. "They are all happy together. He wants you to know that."

I looked at Bill like he'd lost his mind. "What are you talking about?" I asked. "I have four kids – and they are all alive."

"No," Bill said. "He's with two boys. He says they are yours."

Suddenly my heart pounded rapidly and I got a lump in my throat. I couldn't speak.

My husband and I had already had three children when I

became pregnant again – with triplets. But two of them died early in my pregnancy. Our sadness at the time was overwhelming, but my husband and I had never talked about them much after we got the devastating news from the doctor. We felt blessed that one survived, and we focused all our energy on him. We didn't even know the sex of the two who had died...until Grandpa told me.

"Two more sons?" I said as the tears flowed. Many people didn't even know we'd lost two babies. It was so personal, and stored so deep in the archives of my mind, that it didn't immediately register with me who the two boys he was with could have been.

To my husband and me, they had never had faces, but to Grandpa they did. They were his now – and that made me very happy.

"He wants you to know they are in good hands," Bill said. "He says all three of them are always watching over you and your family."

I finally got my closure – plus some.

Lynn

Chapter 11

VALIDATING

Spirits will often make their presence known in subtle, but direct, ways that we can understand on a personal level. We need to slow down our thoughts and be present to make the connection with them.

The first step in any reading is to validate the name of the spirit who is coming through. Is it a grandma? Grandpa? Child? Grandchild? Parent? Sibling? Friend? Friend of a friend? For me, this is one of the most exciting parts of a reading and definitely the most exciting for the client. Many first-time clients have some skepticism about my abilities. That's perfectly fine — I expect that. In fact, I like it when they do, because it makes watching that skepticism wash away as I validate the identity of the spirit even more satisfying. But for clients, the feeling of validation goes well beyond "satisfying." Their exhilaration makes their hearts flutter and bodies tremble. If you have never had a reading from me or another legitimate medium, imagine being in that position for a moment. One minute you are thinking to yourself, *I wonder if this will work. I wonder if a spirit of someone I know will really come through. I wonder if this medium is for real.* The next minute, there is no turning back. The spirit is here and has been validated, you realize this is real, and the excitement begins as we listen to what the spirit has to say.

I tell everyone who schedules a reading with me to be sure to come in with one thing above all else: an open mind. You don't need to meditate like I do (though meditation wouldn't be a bad idea if you have the chance), but you should be open to the possibility that anything can happen and that anyone can come through. Again, skepticism is fine; the spirits and I can handle that. But if you come in with a completely closed mind, you will miss out on a wonderful opportunity. The purpose of your reading should be to connect with someone who has passed on, with the hope that you will leave with more love, more peace, more comfort, more closure. That won't happen if you aren't open to the possibilities.

Also, I ask clients to understand my role in this venture: I am the messenger trying to connect you (someone I don't know) with a spirit (also someone I don't know). When it comes to confirming the identity of a spirit who is present, that validation rests heavily on your shoulders. Usually, the only thing I know about you, if you schedule a private reading, is your name. And if I'm giving you a reading in front of an audience in an auditorium or some other large venue, I don't even know that. So if I say, "A spirit whose name starts with a *J* is coming through," be open to anyone you knew who died and whose name begins with that letter. Yes, the information will be general at first, but the spirit will become more specific as we go, and we will soon know if it is the person you are thinking of or not. Be open from the start and see what unfolds.

I once told a highly skeptical woman I was reading for that I felt as if her husband was coming through, and that he had recently passed at a young age. She confirmed that he had died young.

I then got more specific, asking her if he would be fifty-three years old now. She got that "Aha! You're wrong," look on her face that I've seen on occasion from skeptics.

"No," she said, "that's not him. He wouldn't have been fifty-three until later this year."

Haha! Okay, how about cutting me — and her husband — some slack! Remember, this is not a black-and-white process. I knew it was him as soon as she said that, and he helped me reverse her thinking by giving me more information about specific moments between the two of them that validated without a doubt for her that he was with us.

There are also many times when validations are convincing right off the bat, because some spirits start conveying specific details as soon as we begin. For example, I once read for a woman whose friend was coming through. He didn't give me an initial or name. What he did give me was the image of the car belonging to movie icon James Bond. I then continually heard James Bond's famous line "Bond — James Bond." I chuckled at these messages, but trusted that they would mean something to this woman. When I told her about the car and said the line, she cried.

"My friend's name was James," she said. "He drove a sports car that he was in love with, and he also loved James Bond movies. Every time he would talk about that car, he'd say that line with his name: Smith — James Smith." That quickly and easily validated for both of us that her friend was present, given how specific and personal this detail was.

In 2014, during one of my readings in front of an audience, I was focusing on a woman there whose mother and brother were coming through. After they had provided her with some information about them, another spirit jumped in. He was prompting me to speak to the man sitting next to the woman.

"Have you lost someone significant in your life?" I asked him. "Someone with a *B* name? Now I'm hearing *B-r*. It's *B-r*, and ends with an *n*. Maybe Brendan? Or Brandon?"

"My father died. His name was Brian," the man said. The validations continued as I went into tremendous detail about conversations the father and son had years ago. All this combined would have been validation enough, but this spirit seemed determined to leave no doubt whatsoever as he flashed me an unusual image.

"I'm seeing a watch in a collector's safe," I said, referring to one of those small, steel safes that you often find in hotel rooms nowadays to store your valuables in. "Does that make sense?"

The gentleman was so shocked that he struggled to speak. "Yes . . . it was a watch my dad left behind, and the only thing of significance that belonged to him that I kept. I keep it in a safe at home."

And that wasn't even the best part. "He's telling me more," I said. "I'm seeing the number 620." Since we were talking about a watch, I assumed that 620 referred to the time. Maybe the hands of the watch were stuck on 6:20, or maybe his dad died at 6:20. But it had nothing to do with time. The man's jaw dropped when I revealed those numbers.

"That's . . . that's the combination to the safe," he said.

After giving the man a moment to take all this in, I told him that his father wanted him to know that he loved him — something his father had rarely said to him when he was alive.

The emotional reading with that man continued for quite a while. His grandfather later came through, which was followed by a tingling in my spine. The father and grandfather wanted the man to know he should not have the back surgery he was thinking of having — that the quality of his life would be better without it. The man acknowledged that he had a spinal condition and was mulling the option of surgery.

I would guess that after his reading he probably opted not to have it, or at least did more research on it before making a decision.

Look at how that reading unfolded: I was able to channel the letters *B*, *r*, and *n* in an attempt to begin the validation of the spirit, mention the one thing the man kept that had belonged to his father, tell him where he kept it, and even give him the combination to the safe. I then had a message about his future by way of clairsentience, with the tingling in my spine. And it all started with a general and simple question: "Have you lost someone significant in your life?" Who hasn't? But from there, it evolved into a highly specific reading that even gave him some insight into his future, all because his mind was open to the possibilities that spirits could bring to him through me.

An open mind: bring it with you to a reading, and keep it with you throughout the process. Once we have validated who is coming through, the energy will build, and messages from the spirit will become more specific. Then we can begin to interpret those messages.

Over the Rainbow

One of my friends saw Bill on a TV talk show in 2014, and knowing that I had been struggling with the loss of my grandmother, she suggested I look into getting a reading from him. I went online and watched a couple of his clips. What I liked was the way he talked with people. He had such a kind heart. Everything he was trying to do was aimed at bringing peace to people. That appealed to me, so I decided to give it a shot.

Let me first be clear about one thing: as hopeful as I was that Bill could provide me with the comfort I needed, I went in with a healthy amount of skepticism. I am an educated woman, and I don't take much at face value. If he was going to tell me my grandmother was coming through, I was going to need a lot of validation.

Since I lived so far away from Bill, I set up the reading over Skype. That made me skeptical right out of the gate. How can you get a sense of someone over Skype? Well, I don't know how – but he did.

To put the validations I received in order of significance or according to how amazing they are is difficult, because every single one was absolutely unbelievable. He started by saying I was going to be getting married soon. True, though anybody could have seen my ring and guessed that. But then came the immediate confirmation for me that my grandma was with us.

"She is singing 'Over the Rainbow,'" Bill said. "What does that mean?"

"What?" I exclaimed. My fiancé and I were planning a secret civil ceremony with no guests. It was going to be just the two of us – not even a best man and maid of honor. The week before I met with Bill, I downloaded about ten different versions of "Over the Rainbow," which I intended to play at the ceremony. I had told nobody about that! Not a soul – yet there was obviously a soul who knew.

The second validation regarded the little girl I didn't have – yet. Many women will tell you that they quietly pick the names of their future children, even well before they meet their husbands. It's just a woman thing. Well, as my reading continued, Bill asked me who Amanda was. That was the name I had secretly picked out, probably ten years earlier, for my future daughter. I never told anybody – not even my fiancé. I told Bill I had no idea who she was. He asked if I was pregnant or had ever miscarried. I told him no on both counts.

"Well, then, I can't figure this out," Bill said. "She is stuck by your side. Her presence is so strong. There is no doubt she will eventually come into your life."

It wasn't like he was fishing for names. He literally said "a little girl named Amanda." I will have to stay tuned for that one – but I have no doubt she will be coming.

He also said he saw an image of ducks being fed. That one took me back to my childhood. When I was little, Grandma and I used to save every crumb of leftover bread, freeze it all, then defrost it a day in advance of going to the park to feed the ducks. I even have a photo of us doing it – that's how significant the event was to us.

The last thing Bill brought up, and the primary reason my grandma came to communicate with me, was my family. After Grandma died, things happened between her children that were just horrendous. There was so much fighting and arguing over her estate, and so many relationships were broken. Bill brought up a lot of names and issues that few people knew about – and one that absolutely floored me. I was supposed to get my grandma's house after she passed, but one of her daughters sold it out from under me. I was so angry, and devastated, because that house was what I considered home. My grandma had lived there forever. It meant a lot to her, and to me.

"Your grandma wants you to know that the house wasn't

important," Bill said. I was blown away. I hadn't said a word to him about the house.

"She knows you feel like you let her down, but you didn't," he continued. "She doesn't care about it. She wants you to stop feeling bad and to let it go."

When my reading was finished, I thought of every possible way Bill could have known in advance about these things – Facebook, Twitter, Google. What had I put out there? What had others put out there? The answer was: absolutely none of it. Not even a private investigator could have known about a lot of that stuff – the song at my wedding ceremony, the name I wanted for my future daughter, my feelings about the house. These weren't just secret things but private thoughts I held within my heart, deep in my soul, that nobody here on earth knew.

I think it's natural, going into a reading with a medium, to ask yourself if it's real or not. But if you can get yourself past that, the reading can be cathartic. With Bill, you will find that very easy to do.

Dawn

Chapter 12

INTERPRETING

When we ask for something, it is usually right in front of us; but when it is not presented as we had imagined it would be, we ignore it. Be aware of what is before you, and recognize the answer to your prayer.

hesitate to tell this story. The language in it and my embarrassment at what I did still make me cringe, but I feel compelled to share it because it's the best lesson I have ever learned in relation to interpreting information that spirits give me. Fortunately, I also have a sense of humor genuine enough that I can laugh at my gaffes.

One day early in my career, a woman came to my office for a reading. As is the case with most of my first-time clients, I had never met her before and knew absolutely nothing about her, aside from her name. I had no idea why she had booked me for a reading — whether she just wanted to try it for fun or was hoping to connect with someone in particular. Within a couple of minutes after our session started, I felt the strong presence of a male spirit in the room. But there was a problem. This man appeared to be calling himself a derogatory name. Specifically, it seemed like he was calling himself a dick.

It's perfectly fine to laugh. I still do every time I think about it. At the time, though, I didn't find it very funny. In fact, it was downright unnerving because I wasn't experienced enough to know how to handle such a validation. It put me in an awkward situation. I had never encountered a spirit using language like that. I kept trying, in my mind, to ask him for another sign as I repeatedly heard the word *dick*. I didn't want the woman to know what he was saying.

Is there any other way you can identify yourself? I kept asking him in my mind. *Please? Pleeeease?* But he was belligerent, refusing to give me any more hints.

Now it may appear that the logical thing for me to have done was to assume he was trying to say his name was Dick, but the information was being presented to me in such a way that I felt confident he was giving me an insight into his personality. It was similar to the way Eric, whom I mentioned earlier, was trying to tell me who he was through sarcasm. The thought of this spirit's actual name being Dick was not even part of my thought process.

So what did I do? The worst thing I could have done. Rather than just saying the word *dick* and letting her try to validate for me who it might be, I gave her my own interpretation. "I'm getting a man coming through, but I don't know his name. All he seems to be telling me is that he was a dick in life," I said with trepidation.

Fortunately, she didn't get angry. In fact, her eyes lit up as she laughed. "No, no, no!" she said. "I know who you're talking about! His name is Dick!"

Lesson learned: convey the information and let the client try to validate who it is before trying to interpret it myself.

I trusted myself with the information I received — I knew what he was saying — but I took it too far. I should have presented the word to her first, then tried to help her interpret it if it didn't resonate with her. I should have simply said, "Does the word *dick* mean anything to you?" Of course, that itself may not sound like such a great thing when presented like that; but to her it would have made perfect sense, since someone close to her who was deceased had that name.

I learned from that reading that my primary responsibility as a medium is to simply relay information, while it is the job of the people I am reading for to validate that information. They knew the spirits when those individuals were alive; I did not. I cannot assume anything, and I have to trust that my client will be able to lead the interpretation. As it turned out, Dick wasn't a dick at all. He was just a nice guy named Dick . . . who had to seriously be wondering why he selected me as his messenger.

In another example from early in my career, I gave a reading to a mother whose son had recently died of leukemia. Her daughter, the boy's sister, was also there. Throughout the reading I kept receiving an image of plums. The image did not fit with any of the other images I was seeing, so I was hesitant to say anything; it seemed awkward. After the boy flashed the image for the third time, I finally relented.

"This seems ridiculous," I said, "but he keeps showing me plums. I don't know if that means anything to either of you, but I feel like he really wants me to share that."

The mother and daughter started to cry. "The last few days of his life, all he wanted to eat were plums," his mother said. "We would put small pieces of them to his lips and feed him." It was the very last food he ate, and the family still had a couple crates of plums at home because of how much he had wanted them. Something that seemed ridiculous to me made perfect sense to the mother and daughter. Had I continued to resist the image and not let them do the interpreting, they never would have experienced that clear validation that their son and brother was with us.

The most difficulty I have when it comes to interpretation is with numbers, which are thrown at me in nearly every reading. In the example of the man I spoke of earlier who had his father's old watch, I assumed "620" had to do with time. But it had nothing to do with that and was instead the combination to the safe where he kept the watch. If I see the number ten, it could mean something happened to the spirit when she was ten years old, or that there is something related to her regarding the month of October, the tenth month of the year. But the reality could be that she had ten children and is trying to get a message to her tenth child, or that she had a child who was an athlete and wore the number ten. You can see how different those interpretations are. They are all over the spectrum. That is why I have to let my client come up with possible meanings before I do so; often the spirit will give me a "yea" or "nay" as we discuss the possibilities.

I realize cynics will say that any number can mean something to everyone. Of course that's true. If I tell you a spirit is giving me the number seven, I bet it could mean something to you, even something fairly significant, if you think about it long enough. Consider all those in your life who have passed. Was one of them born in July, or on the seventh day of a month? Did they have seven children? Was seven their lucky number? Did something noteworthy happen to them when they were seven years old? But as I mentioned in the previous chapter, keep an open mind, let the reading evolve, and the spirit will get more specific. The reading has to start somewhere, and numbers or letters are a frequent starting point for the spirits.

One thing people must be careful about is interpreting information too literally. A perfect example of that is the time when I told a woman that a spirit was warning me her husband was going to have a stroke in a few months (which is another topic I will soon address — conveying bad news). The date for the stroke that kept coming to me was April 6. I gave her that date and, from what I later deduced, she pretty much circled it on her calendar. Well, April 6 came and went without any problems. However, two days later, on April 8, he suffered a stroke. Guess who received the brunt of her anger? The next time she saw me, she chastised me for missing the date.

I thought, *Are you kidding me? Three months in advance, I come within two days of a major medical issue, and this is my fault? Or the spirit's fault?* This is much like the earlier instance in which a woman verified that her husband had died, but said he would not have been fifty-three years old at the present date, despite what I felt her husband's spirit telling me. She said that what would have been his fifty-third birthday was still a few months away. Don't forget my belief that time does not exist in the spirit realm the same way it does here. There are no clocks or calendars on the other side. For that reason, I don't believe it is easy for spirits to send me messages that relate to earthly time. I use my senses to give as accurate of a time frame as I possibly can, but it's certainly not an exact science.

Something else to keep in mind is that interpreting information from spirits is like interpreting anything else in this world. Ten people can watch an interview with someone, and each can come up with a different interpretation of what that person said, because each of us is different. We have different backgrounds, experiences, and beliefs that contribute to our interpretations and conclusions. My advice to people I do readings for is this: believe in the information you receive from me, just as I believe in the information as it comes to me from the spirits, but understand that there is some wiggle room and the need for you to use your own brain. Imagine being one of these spirits, with no audible voice, no hands, no face. Now try communicating what you want to say. It's not easy. I believe they do the best they can with what they have. I assume that they can communicate with each other over there perfectly fine. But when they are trying to communicate with those outside their world, it's a challenge.

Keep your mind open, do not come in with expectations, and know this communication process is not exact. The spirits are working hard to get their messages to you — work with them to make that happen.

And no matter how well you or I interpret a message from a spirit, always remember one very important fact: you are in control of your life. Not me and not a spirit. Your decisions are ultimately what will rule the direction in which your life goes. God gave us the ability to choose our paths. Yes, outside circumstances can alter the courses of our lives, such as when someone does something unexpected (good or bad) to us or for us. But when I tell you what a spirit is saying, do not assume it is automatically gold.

If I am told by a spirit that a stroke is coming your way on April 6, you probably should not wait to see if you make it through that date or believe you are in the clear if you do, and then blame me for being wrong. You may instead want to review your health history and the lifestyle you have been living, and decide if it would make sense for you to go in for a checkup.

On the flip side, a spirit may not tell you something specific that will happen in your life, or something specific that you should do, but may simply open the door for you to make changes that will better your life or the life of someone else. Don't wait for the spirit to give you point-by-point instructions on what to do next. Let the spirit's guidance help you use the mind God gave you.

I cannot tell you with 100 percent certainty what will or will not happen to you. My job is to be a conduit, to provide information from a spirit who is trying to guide or comfort you in an attempt to make your time here on earth better.

Choosing to Forgive

My reading with Bill in 2010 was nearly canceled. It was one of the first out-of-town group shows he'd ever done, before anyone really knew who he was. Only a few of us attended. He decided to go ahead with it anyway because he said there was a reason he was supposed to do it — and that I was the reason.

Bill and I had never met. We lived two thousand miles apart, and there was no particular spirit I wanted to connect with. Yet he knew I was the reason? I didn't know what to think about that — until my late uncle came through.

I didn't like my uncle, and that's putting it mildly. I harbored so much anger because of him when he was alive, and it remained after his death. He had problems with alcohol, which created a lot of tension within our family. He selfishly pulled a lot of resources from us — our time, our money — and I resented him for that. My anger was scathing.

When Bill told me my uncle was present and confirmed it with several validations of facts about my uncle known to nobody but my family and me, I started to shake and cry. My emotions were overwhelming. I was angry that my uncle had come through to communicate with me. After all of the pain he inflicted on me when he was alive, he thought it was okay to come back in death? I never imagined he would show up, and I didn't want to hear anything he had to say — but his presence was too strong for Bill to ignore.

Well it's so nice that you're here, I sarcastically said to my uncle in my mind. *The least you could do is apologize.*

About three seconds after that, while Bill was in the middle of saying something else, he stopped his thought — as if he'd been interrupted with another thought. "Your uncle says he wants to apologize to you," Bill said. "He is sorry for all of the pain he caused you and the family."

This revelation sent chills down my spine. Bill was talking about something else when my uncle interrupted him to apologize – seconds after I told my uncle in my mind that he should apologize!

That reading gave me the guidance I needed to change the course of my life. Over the next few years, I gave up the partying lifestyle completely. I had been similar to my uncle in that respect – and I did not want to end up like him. I also got into a relationship with a man, well after my reading with Bill, who had his own battles with alcohol. That evening with Bill and the connection he made with my uncle were still fresh in my mind when I met my boyfriend, and they enabled me to better understand what my boyfriend was going through and to get him the help he needed.

The best way I can describe what Bill did for me is to say that he opened doors that had been locked. I have made a lot of changes in my life – in what I do and in the way I think – because of what happened at that reading. Bill didn't tell me what to do with my life. He, along with my uncle, gave me the spiritual guidance I needed in order to take control of my destiny and turn things around.

That new attitude also gave me the ability to forgive my uncle. It didn't happen overnight. It took a lot of time to release years of hatred, but I eventually did it. I don't know if it helped my uncle at all, considering he is already on the other side, but it certainly gave me a freedom I hadn't felt in years – and it ultimately has made me a better person.

Laura

Chapter 13

CONVEYING

The best way to bring peace to those around you is by example – live a life of peace.

One thing I've learned through my journey as a psychic medium is how to properly and respectfully convey information that I receive from the spirits, which isn't always easy. The two issues that I most need to be careful with are those involving health and relationships, especially romantic relationships.

When it comes to people's health, consider the instance when I warned the woman her husband would likely have a stroke. While the spirit was correct about the stroke, and while I conveyed the proper information to her, I didn't feel right after I told her. It was one of my early readings, and I was inexperienced in conveying such bad news. I felt at the time that telling her was the right thing to do — and, without a doubt, it was — but how I conveyed it to her needed some tweaking. There are right and wrong ways to break news to people. Given how upset she was because the date I gave her for the stroke was off by two days, I decided to rethink how I dealt with such news.

It's not that I now filter the meaning of a negative message;

it's simply that I present it more sensitively. If I were to get in the way of the information itself because I think someone shouldn't be given bad news, then I would be inhibiting the pure messages and validations that come from the spirits. To not tell the woman that I saw a stroke would befall her husband would have been wrong. But there were better ways to share the information.

Let's say a spirit were to show me that a client would be involved in a horrific car accident. I wouldn't say, "I see you getting in a horrific car accident." To do so would be insensitive. I don't want a person to have a heart attack and die during the reading because I stressed him out. Another reason is because, in making that prediction, I would cross the "interpretation" line. I don't actually know if the accident has already happened or simply might happen. So I may start by saying, "Were you in a car accident recently?" If the client says yes, then the information can be viewed as a validation because the spirit was acknowledging an accident that already happened. Issue averted. If the answer is no, I may say, "You really need to be careful while driving."

I may also ask the person to understand that his loved ones are worried about him driving, that they are trying to protect him when he's on the road, and that he needs to be extra careful and protect himself. In this way, I use the spirit's guidance to make the person conscious of his driving and encourage him to change his driving habits — by driving at a lower speed, not driving after drinking, or not driving when the weather is bad. And, hopefully, I've prevented him from worrying that an accident is inevitable.

At a show I did in Los Angeles, I got messages from a spirit for a woman sitting in the audience. A friend of hers came through first, followed by her father. I received several signs that firmly validated for her that it was those two who were present.

When I thought the reading was finished, I turned and walked back toward the center of the stage. Her father interrupted to give me another message, this one about her health. He told me that she might have cancer. He said she would be okay, but that she needed to get it taken care of. I stopped as that message came through and turned back to the woman. I thought for a moment about how to address it. Coldly saying, "Oh, one more thing . . . your dad is telling me you have cancer" was something that might have come from the mouth of the young and inexperienced Bill. I knew better now.

"Have you been sick?" I asked her.

"Sick? No, not at all," she said.

"You're sure?" I asked, trying to get her to really think hard about her recent health. "Nothing around your stomach area?"

"Positive," she replied confidently.

"Okay," I said as I started to turn back toward center stage again. "But you should probably have yourself checked out. Your father says there may be an issue you need to address." Sensitive — but getting the point across (and you will read about the stunning conclusion to her story in the next chapter).

At another show I did, the spirit of the mother of a woman in the audience came through. The mother wanted to talk about her daughter's health and did so through clairsentience; I felt her putting pressure on my lungs. The pressure was so strong that I became alarmed about this woman's life. Rather than scaring her by directly bringing her mortality into it, I said, "Your mom really wants you to keep an eye on your lungs; she says you know what to do — you just have to do it."

The woman validated the information, saying that she had bad asthma and was having issues with her lungs because she was also a smoker. So the message was correct; I conveyed it in a sensitive way, making the urgency of the situation clear to everyone, and now it was up to her to do something about it.

In the case of the woman whose husband had the stroke on April 8, it's clear to me now that giving a specific date wasn't the best idea, even though my intentions were good. A better way to handle it would have been to question her about her husband's health in general, then suggest he go to a doctor within a week or two — whatever time frame would be well in advance of the specific date I was given. A clear and urgent, yet sensitive, message that would have encouraged her husband to take care of the issue, but without sending anyone into a frenzy.

The second main issue that I mentioned I need to be sensitive about when conveying information is relationships, specifically those involving romance. Spirits are often responsible for getting two people together. They like to play matchmaker, in a sense, by aligning events so that two people's paths cross — but this may not happen if we humans know too much.

I've already talked about a spirit who orchestrated a non-romantic relationship. Remember the story about Michael trying to get messages to his mother, Kimberly? Think about how that unfolded: Rachel and I were friends; I gave Rachel a reading involving two people she didn't know, named Michael and Kimberly; of all the accountants Kimberly could have gone to for her taxes, she chose Rachel, within about a week after the reading; and Kimberly happened to be the mother of Michael. If you think that was all coincidence, I have a beautiful ocean here on the California coast for sale, if you're interested.

It was Michael who orchestrated it all. Spirits do it all the time, and they also do it to bring people romantically together.

How many times have you heard two romantically linked people talk about fate? There is your fate. The spirits are the ones creating it.

A problem can arise, though, if I convey too much information to the client. We humans can screw up fate with our need-to-know-now attitudes, our lack of patience when it comes to letting life simply unfold as it should — or as the spirits believe it should.

For example, people often come to me for a reading in order to get details about their future love lives — who will they meet, where they will meet, when they will meet? While most of the time I do give them the details I receive, such as initials or names or physical descriptions, I will stop if the person appears desperate and continues to push for more information. In fact, the spirits are often the ones to put an end to the conversation, by showing me a literal stop sign or the color red, their signal to me that it's time to cease. I might say to the client, "I'm being guided now not to tell you anything more, but here is a general timeline of when things might happen" (for example, I may tell them they will meet the person sometime in the following year).

Here is where a problem might arise if I don't stop. Let's say I give you all sorts of wonderful details about the person you are eventually going to meet, all the way down to: "You will meet your future lover one morning in the next month in a Starbucks. His name will be Sam, and he will have brown hair and blue eyes." Guess what you are probably going to do every morning for the next month? Not only will you go to Starbucks, but you will pay attention only to those men with brown hair and blue eyes, and you will probably even try some sneaky methods to find out their names. What you will have done is completely eliminate the power of the reading I did for you. Instead of letting the spirit orchestrate a synchronistic event, you will have hindered that process by taking it upon yourself to make sure it happens. Remember, we all have free will. How you utilize that free will in conjunction with your reading could work for you or against you, depending on your actions.

The main point I want to get across when it comes to the messages I convey during a reading is that I will always be honest with you, but in a compassionate and sensitive way. I believe the spirits utilize me to share their messages because of my compassion and sensitivity. They know that I will give their loved ones messages in a manner that they would use if they were able to be here physically and do it themselves. If the person I am reading for thinks I'm an authoritative jackass, she is not going to feel a connection to me. That could cause her to dismiss anything I tell her, even make her look for reasons to be cynical about me, which would defeat the spirits' purpose in trying to come through. If someone you love smokes too much, would you say, "You really should think about quitting for the good of your health," or would you say, "You need to stop smoking right now before you die?" Most would do the former. Keep in mind, too, that I don't know you or the spirit, so I'm in a bit of an awkward spot. It's not just what I say but also how I say it that matters.

The spirits and I have one common purpose: to bring peace, healing, and hope to you. You've undoubtedly heard the phrase "I'm just the messenger." People often use it to exonerate themselves of responsibility for the issue at hand. Yes, I am just the messenger, but I'm the messenger for a reason: my job is to responsibly convey to you what the spirits on the other side want you to know.

My Daughter's Return

My husband and I have two sons. I have also had twelve miscarriages. Yes, twelve. Every miscarriage happened early in the pregnancy — except one. I had a daughter who died after I carried her for six months. It was a death I could never let go of. Losing a child at any point during a pregnancy is devastating, but when you carry one for six months...I felt selfish and guilty for even trying to have her after all the miscarriages I'd had. I felt so blessed to have our two boys, but the pain in my heart over losing my little girl was always there.

I scheduled a reading with Bill for my mom as a birthday gift to her, and I went along with her. This was about five years after my daughter's death. The reading was lively because my dad and great-grandma came through. Bill then focused on me and said that my great-grandma was watching over all of my lost children, and she especially wanted me to know that she was there with my daughter. Bill had no knowledge of my past complications, or that I had specifically lost a daughter. To hear this was the last thing I expected. It gave me an immediate sense of healing that I hadn't known I desperately needed.

But then Bill became more direct with me. "You need to listen to me," he said. "I know this may be scary to hear, but your great-grandma is insisting that I tell you that you need to let go of the fear and anxiety and stress of being pregnant. She says that this negative energy is not good for you and only makes you sicker."

"I know," I said. "I need to get over everything."

"No, you don't understand," he replied. "You need to let all the negative emotions go and just hold on to faith, because your little girl is coming back."

I was stunned.

"No, that can't happen," I argued. Doctors had diagnosed me with a rare heart condition; getting pregnant again would be life threatening. I knew that everything in the reading to that point was true – the validations were there – but there was no way this could be possible.

I was upset about what Bill had said, but he didn't back down from his claim. Then he said the words that knocked the wind right out of my chest.

"You have dreams about her nightly," he said, continuing to convey words from my great-grandma. "You think about her when you are alone. You feel guilty and sad, but it's not your fault. The reason you can't let her go is because she's supposed to be here."

Even though she'd been gone for five years, I dreamed about her almost every night and thought about her every day. And yet I hadn't told one person – not even my husband – about it. I was mystified. I believed in Bill, and I knew my great-grandma was present with us, but there was no way this could be true.

I went home and told my husband, who also knew another pregnancy was not possible. But two months later, when I took my brother to see Bill for a reading, Bill's first words were that the spirits were saying congratulations to whoever was pregnant with a baby girl.

"Nobody is pregnant," we told him.

"Somebody is," Bill said. "I'm positive."

A few days later, having that same sick feeling I'd had numerous times before, I found out I was, in fact, pregnant. Believe it or not, doctors determined that I had been literally one day pregnant when I saw Bill. And at fourteen weeks, when I had an ultrasound done, we found out it was a girl.

The pregnancy was like all the others – rough and complicated and scary. But I kept reminding myself of the warm thoughts and feelings Bill had conveyed to me from my great-grandma during my reading: let go of the fear, anxiety, and negativity.

And I did. I am so happy to say that we are now a family of five with the recent addition of a very healthy and happy baby girl. Her name is Kenzy — the same name that we gave to our baby girl who died.

I've always believed there's a place for our souls on the other side, and that spirits watch over us, but I never knew they are *always* there and know our internal conflicts. What happened during and after my reading gave me a new understanding of what spirits can do and how they are involved in our lives. And because of that involvement, I miraculously became a mother again.

Kristy

Chapter 14

KEEP THAT with YOU

Surrender all your worries to God, be patient, and the clarity you are seeking will become evident.

No two readings are ever alike, for obvious reasons. But one line nearly everyone will hear from me at some point during a reading, whether it is a private one or in a group setting, is "keep that with you." Many times a spirit will give me a message that pertains to something that will happen in the future, or that has already happened but which the client is unaware happened, or that has already happened but the client does not immediately remember. Rather than dismissing that message because the person does not know what I am talking about, I have to trust what the spirit is telling me and believe there is a significant reason why the spirit wants my client to know about it. So when I say "keep that with you," it means to remember that we talked about it and to watch for something related to it to eventually be disclosed.

One example of this is a reading I did for a woman named Shannon in Southern California, who was looking for some direction in her life. Her grandma was the spirit coming through to me, but everything her grandma told me made little sense to Shannon. I talked about marriage, even though Shannon was not married or even dating anybody at the time. I mentioned a man named Joshua — she didn't know a Joshua. It appeared even more ridiculous to her when I said this Joshua guy had a scar on his left arm where he'd had surgery. Shannon's grandma also said that her granddaughter would be moving away soon, somewhere between California and Kansas. Shannon had no plans at the time to move.

On the surface, it didn't appear to Shannon to be a stellar reading. But spirits don't make things up. I confidently told her to keep it all with her and see what happens.

Three years after that reading, Shannon stopped into my office...and she wasn't alone. She was with her new husband, Joshua. Joshua proudly rolled up his left sleeve to show me a scar where he'd had surgery. And the newlyweds were only going to be around for a couple more weeks; they were about to move to Utah.

A more complicated and fascinating example of someone keeping my reading with her is that of the woman I mentioned I'd talked to in Los Angeles. At that show, I was told by her father that her health was at risk, that she possibly had cancer and should get herself checked out. Her name was Tracy, and the Los Angeles show was actually the second time she had seen me. She had first seen me at a show two months earlier. At that first show, her father's spirit came through with the numbers four and forty-four directed at Tracy, but she had no idea what they meant. She said she worked at a tavern that had the number four in its name, but I knew that wasn't it. I told her to keep those numbers with her because they definitely pertained to something important.

The morning after the second show Tracy attended, the one in which I addressed her health, she woke up feeling sick. "I went into the bathroom and started hemorrhaging," Tracy recalled while later telling me the story. "I had blood all over my legs."

She drove herself to a hospital, where tests revealed a tumor on her uterus. Doctors had to do an emergency hysterectomy. After surgery, one of the doctors told Tracy specifically what he found. "We pulled out forty-four lymph nodes," he said. "Four of them were cancerous."

"My reaction?" Tracy said with a laugh. "Oh...my...God!"

She had had to keep the information about those numbers with her for two months, but she ultimately found out what they meant. Yes, it would have been ideal if the messages could have been reversed — if her father could have clearly revealed the potential health issue at the first show, then the numbers at the second show. But spirits work the way they do for a reason. It's possible her father simply couldn't muster enough energy to get all of the information through at that first show, or that I was interrupted by another spirit before he could tell me everything he wanted to tell me. Whatever the case, everything was validated in the end. It just took some time.

The "keep that with you" line is your cue that you have "spirit homework," which I talked about earlier. Remember the story about Dakota, and that when I told her someone in her family named Daniel was murdered, she denied it? She mentioned it to her mom later that day, who knew exactly who Daniel was. I don't know if I specifically told Dakota to keep that information with her, but that would have been a typical "keep that with you" situation. A message that you keep with you could also refer to something that hasn't even happened yet, such as in Tracy's case. So you cannot actually do any homework in that situation, but you do need to keep your eyes and ears open for that particular circumstance to eventually be revealed. It could be, for example, a health issue, pregnancy, change in job status, change in relationship status, or relocation. As I mentioned earlier, it could also be something that has already happened and that you know about, but that you simply cannot remember at the time of the reading. If you keep the message with you long enough, eventually the circumstances that it relates to will come to mind and the message will make sense.

As you know by now, when spirits see an opportunity to communicate with their loved ones through me, they do not hesitate to leap at the chance, nor do they hold much back, which is why I usually have to say "keep that with you" at some point during every reading. They know this may be their one chance to reach their loved ones. If they feel they must download everything in one shot, they will, even if it applies to the future and doesn't appear to make sense now.

Also remember that, as I believe, there are likely no clocks or calendars where the spirits are. They are good at giving me numbers, but not always good at telling me the meanings or the units of measurement of those numbers. They may tell me something that could manifest in three days — or three years. When I did one of my early readings for my friend Rachel, I told her a spirit was showing me that she was going to move back to her hometown, and it had something to do with the number six. My interpretation was that she would be moving within six months. It was a place where she hadn't lived in thirty years, so it didn't seem possible to her. Long story short: Rachel did move back to her hometown — six *years* later.

I didn't interpret it correctly, but it taught me a valuable lesson about how this whole communication thing with spirits works: as long as we trust the messages we receive from them and keep those messages with us, chances are very good that they will all eventually make sense.

Singing for Mom

I was part of an audience at one of Bill's shows in 2013. It was nearing the end when Bill said one more spirit was trying to squeeze through.

"I think we saved the best for last," he said. "I don't know who this spirit is for, but I know she belongs to someone in this top row." He was pointing to my row.

"The spirit's name is Jan...Janice...Janet..."

I got chills as I raised my hand. It was my mom, Jan. Bill immediately gave me several details that validated her identity. One of the funniest was when he asked if I had changed the color of my hair. "Yes," I said.

"Well, your mom doesn't like it," he said.

"Well, I didn't like her hair blonde," I replied, getting a good laugh from the audience. This was so like my mom and me. She was always the butt of my jokes, and we used to banter like this all the time. I forgot how much I missed it. I thought, *My gosh, I went from wanting to talk to my mom to getting in an argument with her about our hair colors!* And I was loving every moment of it.

One fascinating moment in the reading was when Bill asked if I was a singer. "No," I said, "but my mom always liked to think I could sing."

"She says she heard you singing," Bill said.

I wasn't sure what that meant. Was she referring to a time during my childhood? Or something else?

"It was something more recent," Bill said. "Keep that with you. You will figure it out."

A full year after that reading, I was thinking about my mom and recalling the day she died. It was a long and difficult day. She had been on life support, and we were about to remove her from it. I

174

called a friend and asked her to add a selection of uplifting songs to her phone and bring it to the hospital. I wanted to play the songs after we took Mom off support so that she could die with the comfort of music.

But when the music finished playing, she was still alive. I had assumed that once she was removed from the machines, she would pass to the other side almost instantly – but she didn't.

Not exactly sure what to do at that point, my friend and I replayed the songs – but, this second time around, in almost a hushed tone I sang along with the music. I don't know why it took me a year to remember that, but I was so glad I did. I don't know that my mom really enjoyed my singing, but it was nice to realize that even as she was dying and appeared to be unconscious, she could still hear me.

My reading with Bill was a surreal experience, as I'm sure it is for most people. You learn that it's not a game – you are really with your mom or dad or whoever is coming through. Then it's comforting, and maybe even funny if your mom is going to give you her opinion about your hair. Then when it's over, you come back to earth and realize you cannot communicate with them in that manner anymore. That's not an easy moment to swallow, but it makes you appreciate what just happened even more.

The time during the reading is a great reprieve. And if you keep a lot of what Bill says with you, you will continue to get those reprieves, which will continue to warm your heart.

Amy

PART III

The Medium Life

Chapter 15

WHY ME?

Let go of the past and be present in the moment to make space for a prosperous future. Reach for the stars and know that anything is possible if you believe it is.

When the spirits were coming to me in the early years during the discovery stage of this gift, I never stopped asking, "Why me?" Seriously, why me instead of any other person on the planet? Why not a friend? A relative? Someone more religious? Someone closer to God? Someone who actually wanted to be a psychic or medium but never had the ability?

In those first few years, I tried to deny that it was happening. It was too "out there." Too crazy. Not possible. And even when I did finally accept that it was real and that there was no escaping it, I had difficulty determining if it was actually a blessing or a curse. When spirits are beating on your brain nonstop, trying to get through to their loved ones — as I will discuss further in the next chapter — it is not easy to deal with. If it was a blessing to be able to connect people here to those on the other side, what did I do to deserve such a blessing? If it was a curse to have this pandemonium in my head every day, what did I do to deserve such a curse? As time went on, the scale tipped heavily to the blessing side because of all the potential goodness I knew could come from the connections.

I think the first time I truly realized how fortunate I was to have this gift was when I was a student at the conservatory and did the reading for the opera singer who lived on the East Coast. She was the one who had been married to a tenor who had passed away, and the one I said would eventually move to San Francisco and work at the conservatory.

She was one of the first people my voice teacher had me read for, and it couldn't have gone better. She was moved to tears the first time I brought her husband through. It was such a powerful moment for both of us that I realized I should probably be doing readings more often. Part of what made it so powerful for me was her status within the opera industry. Students at the conservatory deeply admired her because of her talent. She was a star to us, someone we all wanted to be like one day. Yet *she* was admiring *me* because of *my* abilities as a medium. She couldn't stop asking me questions, came back to me multiple times for more readings, and encouraged me to continue doing readings for others. Having someone I admired, because of her gift, validate my gift was such an honor, and it helped me recognize that the door to my gift needed to remain open.

But that still didn't answer the question "Why me?"

Being a medium is difficult, primarily because what I do does not involve anything tangible. I cannot see the spirits. They do not make themselves visible during my readings. Their actual voices cannot be heard. I have to fully trust what they are conveying to me, even if I have a client on the other side of the table or people in the audience looking at me as if I have two heads because they are unable to immediately interpret what the spirits are trying to say.

Part of my struggle early on was that I had a preconceived notion of what connecting to the other side was supposed to look like. That's because around the time my mom died, the movie *The Sixth Sense* came out. In that movie, the spirits appeared in the flesh to the little boy. One example was a scene toward the end of the movie when there was a traffic jam that resulted when a person on a bike was struck and killed. While the boy and his mom were stuck in the traffic, the bicyclist — now dead, and covered in cuts and blood — appeared outside the boy's car window with an ominous stare. It was a gruesome-looking spirit, and a scene that gave me chills at the thought of a spirit doing something like that to me. That was how I used to think spirits would appear to us on earth if they were able to do it.

But that was not at all how my mom appeared to me two days after she died. Instead, she looked beautiful, peaceful, inviting. She looked like someone who was in heaven. I had to erase Hollywood from my mind in that respect and welcome what was right in front of me. The movie was accurate, though — at least from my perspective as a medium — in portraying the spirits: they do not come to me to try to scare me. In fact, it is quite the opposite. They want me to be receptive to them, to realize that they need me, and to understand that I am their channel to their spouses, sons, daughters, parents, and friends, just as the spirits ultimately wanted the boy in the movie to realize.

While I still do not have a definitive answer to my question, I do not ask myself "Why me?" anymore. If I ask any question at all, it is: "Why not me?"

The spirits obviously wanted to choose someone, so why not a guy with the personality and patience to deal with their wishes? Truthfully, I think the spirits try to connect with many people here on earth, giving them signs and hoping they will be receptive. But because most people do not believe spirits can appear, or because they assume that what are signs from spirits are nothing more than coincidences, they close the spirits out.

When the spirits first started tapping into my mind, it was like a job interview for me. I wasn't initially totally open to them, but I also didn't completely shut them out. Eventually, I warmed to their presence. I fit the mold of what they were looking for in order to accomplish their missions. I have always tried to be a compassionate, nonjudgmental, unassuming person. I have always been a spiritual person, someone who prays, who meditates, who believes in God and heaven. The spirits recognized that, and I was hired. Some people in this line of work do not practice spirituality of any kind. They are not compassionate. They do not care about the people they are serving as long as they get their money, or as long as they get the spirits off their backs. I truly care about the healing that comes from my readings, and I believe that doing so is essential to successfully connect the two worlds.

Some clients tell me they haven't always received compassion and sensitivity from other mediums they've been to, and that it can negatively affect their overall experience of connecting with their loved ones. Some mediums, these clients have said, are more like auctioneers — they get the clients in, give them readings, and get them out. I do understand why a medium may feel he or she needs to do it that way — a medium should not get emotionally attached to the client during the reading. If that happens, a medium's own thoughts could take over and ruin the connection with the spirits. If I'm doing a reading for someone and feeling much too sorry about what happened to that person, and I'm getting emotionally too involved, it can interrupt that link with the spirits. But on the flip side, there has to be *some* compassion, *some* sense of concern for the client and the emotions he or she is feeling. Mediums are messengers, but human messengers — not machines.

Doing what I do is not a job to me. It is a calling. I believe the spirits knew I would see it that way in time, and that I would honor them by using this gift of empathy and care for the greater good of humanity. It certainly did take me some time to get there, but I stayed the course on this journey. That is the best answer I have for why I was chosen.

Easing the Guilt

A young man named David who had faced many struggles throughout his short life was shot to death in 2009. The circumstances surrounding his murder inflicted a tremendous amount of guilt and pain on me. He was one of my son's best friends and had even lived with us for a while. I had unofficially adopted him as my own. You can imagine the heartache, suffering, and confusion I felt, as a mother figure to him, when I found out he was gone. There were so many "what if" questions I asked myself.

What if I had remained more involved in his life? What if I had insisted on his moving back in with us? What if I had expressed my concerns to his immediate family?

Within two minutes of starting my reading, Bill told me there was a spirit present. It was David!

David repeatedly thanked me for my love and insisted that he was okay. He even said his head, where he had been shot, was healed. He assured me that there was nothing more I could have done for him, that he was better now, and that I needed to let go of any guilt I felt. I had always believed he was in a better place, but to hear it from him made all the difference in the world.

Bill had not known who I wanted to connect with or the fact that I had ties to anyone who was murdered. And it wasn't just *what* Bill said that made me feel better but also *how* he said it.

His sincerity, compassion, sensitivity, and even humor as we navigated an emotional reading made me smile and realize not only that David was okay but also that it was okay for me to be okay.

What happened to David is something that will never leave me. It's something I will never "get over." I will always feel some guilt, even though David told me not to. I think it's just natural for a human being to feel that way after losing someone so close in such a tragic way, especially someone who, in my heart, was my own son. But by connecting David with me and assuring me that he is whole again — and by doing it in such a gentle and caring manner — Bill helped me to release a lot of negative feelings, bringing some healing to my mind and heart that I never thought possible.

Tammy

Chapter 16

CHAOS in MY HEAD

Remember to breathe. Breathing connects you to your higher self and the divine knowledge you need to get through your day.

Years ago, when the president of the United States would hold a press conference in the White House, all the members of the media in the room would stand up and raise their hands while shouting "Mr. President! Mr. President!" It was their way of trying to get an edge over one another in an attempt to get him to call on them for the next question. Many movies today still portray White House press conferences that way to add a dramatic effect.

Welcome to the world in my head all day and every day. The spirits often "speak" at once, throwing images or words at me, one after another, as they try to direct me to their loved ones. If I am doing a reading for Jane Doe and spirits connected to Jane Doe's friends know I am reading for her, they will all show up to try to get a message to their loved ones through her. When I pass people on the street, spirits connected to those people rush into my head to try to get me to relay their messages. If I have five individual readings in a day, a spirit connected to the person scheduled for my fifth reading may show up for the first reading because that spirit did not have the patience to wait, and this can certainly cause confusion.

When I am in front of a large audience, I usually have hundreds of spirits trying to come through at once. If I feel a spirit is telling me that his name is John, he is from Boston, and he wants his wife to know that there is money under the mattress, it could actually be three different spirits — one named John, another one from Boston, and another one with money under the mattress — rather than one spirit. And it's my job to figure that out.

In a word, it is chaos.

I usually sense that the spirits would like to cooperate one at a time because they know I will respond better that way. I generally get a message from one, then another, then another, all in a nice, orderly fashion. But bedlam eventually ensues as they all anxiously try to push their messages over each other to me, knowing that my time with their loved ones is limited.

It's like a news show with a panel of four or five people who've come to talk about a political topic. They start out speaking one at a time, but by the end they are all talking over each other, with little mutual respect. They all want to make their points, and they know their time to do so is limited.

Or, using another example from the movie *Ghost*, it is similar to when Patrick Swayze's character visited Whoopi Goldberg's character in her psychic shop. The first time he was by himself. The next time he came, there were several other spirits standing around the table talking at once and driving her crazy as they tried to use her to get through to their family members. Once the spirits learned I have the ability to do what I can do, and that I am willing to do it, word spread among them like wildfire.

This is simply the way it is and, as I have learned from experience, the way it should be. In fact, this could be another way to validate whether the medium you are going to is real or not. If she says that only one spirit is present for the entire reading, she is probably lying. Multiple spirits come through in nearly every reading I give. They may not be the spirits you were hoping to connect with (though they often are), since the spirits are in control of that, but they will definitely be there once that door has been opened.

So how do I deal with the chaos? It's like any other situation: I tune in when I want and tune out when I don't want. The spirits are always there. Their frequency is never turned off. But if I decide I do not want to be bothered by them, I concentrate on something else. I liken it to having a radio on. I can listen intently and jam to the music, or I can do something else while the radio is nothing more than background noise. Don't get me wrong, it's not easy to do. Not only is it difficult to tune the spirits out, simply because of the noise factor, but also it's difficult because I feel some guilt when I do. I have been given this gift and need to use it. People here and spirits there are counting on me. That's why I try to do several readings every day, five or six days a week, if not more.

But I do need downtime, which contributes to the effectiveness of my readings. I need time to meditate, to focus on slowing down my breathing, to elevate my energy level, and to refresh my mind. If I tried to answer every spirit who came to me — which would be impossible given the sheer numbers — my brain would be fried in no time.

Anytime I finish a reading, I am usually mentally drained,

especially after readings in front of large audiences, which can last a couple of hours. My mind often becomes clouded, and it's difficult to remember anything that just happened. It's simply one of the aftereffects of letting the energies of the spirits take over my mind. It reminds me of being in school and pulling an all-nighter while studying for a big exam. You get no sleep, study the same stuff over and over, and memorize everything you can. You are so engrossed in what you are doing that you completely shut out the rest of the world. After you take the test, how do you feel? Even if you did well, you usually aren't in the mood to immediately celebrate. You want to go right to your room and take a long nap to give your mind a break — to give it a chance to refresh itself for whatever is next on your agenda.

Despite some of the challenges my brain goes through as a result of working with spirits, I really and truly love what I do. And the spirits are usually kind enough to let me know that they love what I do. They will often flash me a "thank you" in some form, or send a charge of energy through me after a reading. I know this is their way of showing me that they appreciate what I did.

Yes, I definitely get tired and overwhelmed, but who doesn't when he's doing something he is so passionate about? Some days are frustrating. Most days run smoothly, but I have to expect the unexpected during any reading. I never know what's going to happen, or who might show up. The only guarantee I have is that it's always going to be exciting.

A Family Reunion

People who have been through a reading with Bill like to talk about his accuracy or sensitivity, but there is another element I took away from my brief reading with him that many people may not think about: how much the spirits trust him. I say this based on the number of spirits who came through during my short, thirty-minute reading in the fall of 2014. I was hoping to connect with my father, who had passed ten years earlier – and Dad came through immediately. Bill gave me validation after validation that it was him...but the fun was just getting started.

"Someone named Molly is here with us," Bill said.

"That's my grandmother," I replied.

"And who is Roger?" Bill asked. "Your dad is acknowledging him."

"That's my current husband," I said. "He and Dad never met."

"Well then, who is the *S* name?" Bill wondered. "Is it Steve or Scott?"

"Scott was my first husband."

"Well, he's here now," Bill said. "He wants you to know that he likes Roger and that he watches over him."

I couldn't believe it. Just a few minutes in and I had my dad, grandma, and first husband all in the same room.

Then Bill asked who Lisa was.

"She is my sister-in-law," I said.

"And she is alive, correct?" Bill asked.

"Yes, she is."

"Your father wants you to know that what she is going through right now is not her fault, and he wants you to be active in her life."

I knew exactly what that meant. But there was little time to dissect it, because then Patricia showed up – my second husband's mother, who had died in a car accident. I knew her only for a brief time before she was killed.

"She knows she wasn't in your life long but wants you to know that she has always looked at you as her daughter," Bill said.

And then Lisa's name resurfaced. "I thought you said she is alive," Bill said.

"Yes, she is. She's my sister-in-law," I said.

"Well this is a Lisa who has passed because of something with her neck," he said. It was one of my close friends named Lisa, who had died of melanoma on her neck.

As if all of this wasn't crazy enough, we were about twenty minutes into the reading when the lights in the room started to flicker. Bill laughed and said it was no coincidence. The energy from all of the spirits in the room was causing it. "My gosh," he said. "You have a lot of people over there who want to speak with you."

I don't know how he kept them all straight. It was difficult enough for me to keep them straight, and I knew who they were!

After the thirty-minute reading was over, I walked out of Bill's office carrying a love in my heart that I had never experienced before. My father hadn't left during the reading. I could picture him manning the door, waving the spirits in and sending them over to talk to me.

I went into the reading very nervous, praying that I would get some kind of message from my father. I walked away with far more – a family reunion.

Esther

Chapter 17

WHY NOT YOU?

Have an open mind. Allow yourself to get lost in your imagination. Within that space is your intuition and connection to your higher self.

firmly believe that my ability as a psychic medium is a God-given gift, and that not just anybody can become one simply because he or she wants to. Trust me, I know many people who have tried, and without success. But I do believe all people have some psychic intuition — more than most know they have — that can be cultivated enough to enable them to receive and recognize signs from spirits.

The first step in tapping into that intuition is to set your intention by silently asking the spirits for help when you need it. In other words, pray or meditate. If you are going through a difficult time and are looking for answers or guidance in a particular situation, you first have to ask for help and for signs. That's the easy part. The second step, which is more difficult but equally important, is to open your heart and mind to receiving those signs.

Let's say you are thinking about leaving your job to take one at another company, but you don't know if you should. Pray about it, then keep your eyes and ears open for the answers. What does that mean? Well, chances are pretty good that a random person is not going to walk up to you after you pray and say, "You need to take that job." I have told you how the spirits work — they love to play charades — so you know it's usually not that simple. But if you go out to dinner in the midst of trying to make this decision, and your extremely happy waitress tells you it's her first day on the job, that could be a sign to you that you need to accept your new job. Or if you are watching someone being interviewed on television who comments that the grass is not always greener on the other side, that could be a sign to stay in your current job.

So how do you know whether something is truly a sign? There is no definitive answer to that; you must use your intuition. If you think you have received a sign but aren't confident that it is one, continue to pray and meditate. Ask God for more help, more signs, more assurance, and see what happens.

I have discovered over time that signs intended for me from spirits come in threes. I have heard others say the same. Some of us need to have signs thrown in our faces many times and in different ways before the message resonates with us. So if I were thinking about changing jobs, and the spirits were trying to tell me I should, I might get that sign from the waitress and two other signs totally unrelated to her but related to changing jobs. Maybe the next day I will open a newspaper and find a story about how more Americans are changing careers, and the day after that I will turn on the radio and hear Johnny Paycheck's 1977 country hit "Take This Job and Shove It." Does any station even play that song anymore? I think that would be a huge sign!

Remember, spirits can relay messages in several ways, including through music and humor.

Any time I seek guidance, I look for a white butterfly. To me, that is a sign from my mother. It has been since my late teen years, when I noticed that white butterflies appeared soon after I prayed to my mom for help in certain situations. I am not saying that my mom *is* the butterfly. I am not even necessarily saying that she sent the butterfly. What I am saying is that she directs my attention to one when I ask her for help. It's her way of letting me know that she is listening.

For others, a sign could be a bird or something else in nature. I once did a reading for a woman who lived in a big house in California with picture windows in almost every room. For a week straight a bird tapped on the windows all day long. No matter what room the woman was in, the bird seemed to find her. It became so annoying that she went outside several times to try to shoo it away, but the bird always came back. She even considered calling an exterminator.

At the end of the week, when we had our reading — I knew nothing about her bird problem — I told her that her mother was coming through and showing me a bird. I asked her if she had had any recent encounters with birds. After the woman acknowledged that she had, and commented on how bothersome the bird was, her mother flashed an image of herself throwing her head back and laughing. That bird was the mother's way of letting her daughter know that she was with her. After the reading, the daughter shifted her mind-set, and that annoying bird instantly became a sound and symbol of peace and comfort from someone she loved so dearly. Fortunately, after that discovery, the bird was spared extermination.

Fluctuations in electricity could also be a sign. Spirits are energy currents, so it is easy for them to manipulate electricity and cause cell phones, televisions, computers, and lights to flicker. Yes, when a lightbulb burns out, that could simply mean the lightbulb was old. But if you are sitting on the edge of your bed looking at a photo album, reminiscing about a grandma who has passed, and a light pops off, I would bet it's her letting you know she is there. All spirits are different, and spirits' methods of communicating with you may vary greatly.

Another way they reach us is through music. My mom once told me that when she sang in her school choir her sophomore year, the song they were best known for was "California Dreamin'" by the Mamas and the Papas. During my sophomore year of high school, just a month after Mom passed away and on our first day of choir practice, our director told us to open our binders to the song on the first page — and it was "California Dreamin.'" It's a random song from the 1960s. What were the chances? I definitely took that as a sign that she was with me that day and throughout the year as I came into my own element as a singer.

Some people will argue that the signs I've mentioned are nothing more than coincidences. I understand and respect that opinion but do not agree. I do not believe in coincidences. I believe everything in the universe happens for a specific reason, and that such synchrony is often triggered by spirits. If you are open to that belief, the spirits will be open to giving you the signs and guidance you seek. These will enlighten you to a new way of living and thinking and will empower you to build your own communication system with the spirits. If your mind is closed to the spirits, they will likely recognize your attitude over time and no longer try to communicate with you — which, to me, would be a tremendous opportunity lost.

Here are five spiritual tips I have devised that can help you become more connected, or in tune, with the spirit world in your daily life. They primarily focus on what I have talked about throughout this book: opening your mind and being more aware of what happens around you. Once you master these practices, you will view the world in a different light; peace, healing, and hope will come to you to a degree that previously eluded you.

Understand that our thoughts create our reality. Spirits on the other side are creating and living the lives they wished they could have lived here. The difference is that over there they have no fears or doubts or limitations. Here on earth we are trying to come as close to that as possible, but it's difficult. There are so many physical worries and obstacles that block us from pursuing our passions. We go to work, come home, pay the bills, take care of other responsibilities, then do it all over again the next day. Everyone's struggle is to live in the moment. But on the other side, all they do is live in the moment. Everything they do is their heaven. They might be fishing or painting or doing something else they love. They are doing the things that they wanted to do when they were here but would not let themselves do. The lesson is to stop your negative thinking and reprogram your thoughts. Disrupt your life as it is. Change its pattern. Rather than saying, "I'm sad that I am never going to be able to do this," end that thought process. Use the word *cancel* or *delete* every time you think that way, and start a new way of thinking.

Spiritually cleanse yourself; visualize the clearing of your energy and protect yourself, no matter what your occupation may be. This goes back to realizing that we are spiritual beings inhabiting a physical shell. Just as you take a shower every day to cleanse your body, you must also cleanse your soul each day. Praying is a perfect way to do that. Or follow the meditation I provided near the end of chapter 9, or any of many other meditations you can find in a book or on the internet. Visualize white light coming down from heaven and flowing through your body before ultimately surrounding and protecting you. This is a good time to set your positive intentions for the day. Doing so will help you prevent yourself from absorbing other people's negative junk, which you will undoubtedly encounter throughout the day.

Set your intention that positive life events will unfold, then focus on positive self-talk (affirmations) to help make them happen. Set an intention every day, as if you are planting a seed. Then tell yourself that the universe is going to help you orchestrate the events that will bring that intention to fruition. Everything that happens around you will have something to do with making that intention happen. Let's say you want to lose weight, and you tell yourself when you wake up that morning that you are going to lose weight. Later in the day as you go to the grocery store, you are faced with the temptation to buy the same unhealthy food you have bought in the past. But as you walk in the store you notice a magazine on a rack that shows a gorgeous Hollywood actress who lost fifty pounds. Without your intention, you might not have noticed that picture. Seeing it keeps you on the path toward your goal and motivates you to buy only healthy foods. And this might not have happened had you not set your intention. Setting an intention gets the ball rolling and keeps it rolling throughout the day.

Use the spirit world's help to recognize when you are on the correct path. Understand the synchronicities around you. Do not see anything as coincidence. Spirits who are trying to guide you in the right direction send you signs all day long. Be aware that in the magazine example given earlier, there are two thoughts about the significance of that magazine. One is that it's just a magazine in the front of the store with a picture of another svelte actress who has no bearing on your life. The other is that it is a picture of someone who looks the way you just told yourself that morning you want to look, and it's no coincidence that you noticed it. Whatever it is that you want to do in your life, keep your eyes and ears open for validation that you're doing what you should be doing (or should not be doing). Pay attention to such signs, and trust them.

Grow your own connection to spirits by being open to the signs they show you. I talked earlier about the woman who was annoyed by a bird pecking the windows of her home; she turned that annoyance into a beautiful connection with her mother after I helped her open her eyes and ears and mind. I mentioned that my primary personal connection with my mom is a white butterfly. But that's not the only signal I've received from her. Once when I was struggling with some difficulties, I asked my mom to please show me that she was with me. Around that time, I was driving along the freeway and a car cut me off, nearly causing an accident. I noticed that its license plate was a personalized one that said "Yvonne."

How many people do you know named Yvonne? And there can be no more than fifty of those license plates in this country, right? Guess what my mom's name is? Yes, Yvonne. If I were a cynic with a closed mind, I would have said that was coincidence, or I wouldn't have even noticed the plate. But I had an open mind, and that one small event helped me get through my difficulties; I knew my mom was with me. Remember, do not expect a dead person to appear next to your bed in spirit and tell you what to do. Look instead for the signs they place around you each day.

For the Rest of My Life

My father died tragically in November 2012. He was on a fishing trip in North Carolina with my husband, Matt, and brother-in-law, Chris. They were surf fishing, standing about knee-deep in the ocean, when the undertow caused my dad to lose his balance and go under. As the rough waters pulled him away, Matt and Chris tried desperately to rescue him, but they couldn't. Dad's body was found by fishermen two weeks later, twenty-one miles away.

Losing my dad so suddenly and shockingly was a living nightmare for our entire family — especially for my mom, Virginia. She sought help from many different sources, including a blog dedicated to grieving widows. That was where someone mentioned Bill's name to her.

She asked me and my sister, Kristi, if we would be interested in a reading with Bill to see if we could connect with Dad. We both said yes. It was worth a shot.

The reading was done over the phone, and I couldn't have been more skeptical. It's not that I didn't believe in spirits or that I didn't believe there were people like Bill who could connect with them — I actually did. But when it's your turn to do it, you definitely have your guard up.

A lot of my skepticism subsided immediately, simply because of the manner in which the reading was set up. My mom gave Bill her name, but he did not know Kristi's name or mine. We were each given a conference number to call, so he didn't even know our phone numbers or where we were calling from. He knew nothing about my dad — not how he died, or even that he had died at all. It was about as anonymous as could be.

Bill started with Kristi and mentioned that she was married — a pretty general comment. But the more he spoke, the more specific and personal his reading became. He said Kristi was pregnant and was going to have a girl. It was something we knew, but that she hadn't told anyone outside of our immediate family. He said she would give birth in November, around a date that was significant to all of us. And she did…just a couple of weeks before the two-year anniversary of Dad's death.

Bill then brought up the accident, saying that it was clearly a male presence who was telling him about it. He said that male was "a husband and father." Bill talked about our husbands being with Dad when he died, the fact that it was an accident that happened on the water, and that Dad had drowned.

I am tearing up now as I continue to tell this story, just as I was tearing up during the reading, because after all those validations, Bill gave us eternal comfort with words from Dad to us.

"He wants you to know how sorry he is about what happened, and he's sorry that your husbands were there and had to go through that," Bill said. "He wants them both to know there was nothing they could have done to change the outcome – they did everything they possibly could. He is very proud of them, and he loves all of you."

After several more comments and validations from Dad, Bill left me with this: "He says you were pregnant with his first grandchild when he died. He wants you to know he is honored that you named him after him. Is it Willie? Or William?"

His name is William. Before that point, we had not given Dad's name to Bill.

I can honestly tell you, after having been a huge skeptic, that you cannot sit through a reading with Bill and not believe there is a presence beyond this world. You just can't. You could say that he looks you up in advance, that he Googles you or does something else to find out information about you, but it's not possible. There's just no way. He gets too personal, too deep into your mind, and the result is a healing power beyond anything you can imagine.

Before our reading ended, Bill told us to always keep our hearts and minds open to signs around us that Dad was with us

— specifically, ladybugs. I thought that was odd, given that I hadn't seen a ladybug in years. But sure enough, in 2014, when my husband and I were going through a very stressful time concerning a major family issue that required making several important decisions, a ladybug appeared in the house within a day of each decision we made. We found about six or seven of them in total. The family issue we were dealing with was one in which we definitely would have sought my dad's advice. It was difficult navigating it without him. But seeing a ladybug after each decision was confirmation to us that Dad thought we were doing the right thing.

We never got to say good-bye to my dad. You can never be prepared for such a tragedy. And while we did not get to talk to him through Bill, he got to talk to us. He got to tell us that he was okay and that what had happened to him was okay, ultimately giving us the closure we had been seeking. Dad also assured us that while he is no longer physically here with us, he really is here in spirit all the time — a simple ladybug reminds us of that. We miss him so much, but knowing he is here makes each day a little bit easier.

We all wonder what awaits us after this life. Now I have a sense of what it is. If I were able to have a reading with Bill every day, I would. Since I can't, having one every year — which is how far out Bill was booked when I wrote this — will have to suffice. I will continue to seek his help for the rest of my life. He will always be a significant part of my healing.

Lora

Epilogue

THANK YOU

Live a life of service to others, always show compassion,
and understand that we are all cut from the same fabric.

don't worry about what skeptics say about my gift. I did a little bit when I was younger, but not anymore. That confident
attitude today stems from maturity, experience, the success of
my readings, and the unbelievable support I receive from people
every day in person, on the phone, and through social media.
When you are doing something right, something good, something that is bringing so much joy and happiness to others, nothing else matters.

If you are a skeptic and have made it through this book, I
thank you. As I've said, it's not my desire to change your mind. If
you are a believer now, that's wonderful. If you're still not, that's
perfectly fine, too. I have one mission: to bring peace, healing,
and hope to those who want to connect with their loved ones on
the other side. And with that in mind, I will try to answer some
basic questions that I may not have directly answered yet for
those who may want to believe but still aren't quite sure.

The most common comments I hear from those who have

never been through a reading with me are usually "He must Google everything before a reading" and "I'm sure he went to Facebook to look them up." Of course, anyone who has been through one of my readings will tell you that most of the validations offered by spirits cannot be found in those or similar places. That's the sole purpose of a validation — to provide personal information that proves without a doubt that the spirit is who the spirit claims to be and that he or she is really there. Might a spirit provide a validation that appears on a social media page too? Of course. But that's why the spirit provides numerous validations, one after another, each one more specific than the previous one, and most of which cannot be found anywhere or cannot be known by anyone else.

Many times I don't even know the names of my clients. Someone once informed me that I had done a phone reading for a famous movie star — and I had no idea that I had done it. The star had given me a fake name to protect her privacy. When I found out later that the reading had been for this person, I was told she was blown away by what I was able to reveal to her from the spirits. It was fine that she changed her name. If you want to change your name to protect your privacy, it won't change the fact that the spirits know who you are, and that I will be able to convey their messages to you.

When I'm in front of a live audience or doing readings for callers on a radio show, I never know the names of the people I'm reading for. One of my favorite stories in regard to a live show happened at the 2014 Indiana show I mentioned earlier. I was told by a friend after the show that the man and woman sitting behind her were making sarcastic remarks about me at the start of the show, trying to invalidate anything I said. That doesn't normally happen, but there can always be one or two in any crowd, much like hecklers reacting to a stand-up comedian. As the night and readings went on, and the spirits were leaving a lot of people in awe, the comments from the couple diminished considerably. Then, during the second half of the show, their remarks ceased completely — because their son came through. You would have thought, by all the validations the son gave me, that I must have had a video camera on him throughout his entire life before he died. My friend told me that after I gave the couple their reading, which lasted a good ten to fifteen minutes, the only sound they made the rest of the night was to applaud. It made me happy to hear that, not so much because they had apparently become believers but because their son was able to bring, through me, some peace to their lives.

When I do readings, I encourage clients to record them using video and/or audio. Be wary of a medium who won't let you do that. They should have nothing to hide. From my perspective, clients should be able to refer back to the recordings anytime they need some comfort or validation, or to remember anything I said involving spirit homework or keeping something with them. I've also learned that many people who record their readings use them as a form of meditation, listening to them as they fall asleep at night.

As I start a reading, and as the reading progresses, I make sure clients understand that I want to know as little about them as possible, and that I want them to respond to me succinctly during the reading. For example, if I say that your husband is coming through and that he is showing me a red convertible, I may ask, "Does that make sense to you?" All I want is a "yes" or a "no." I don't need you to tell me why it makes sense. The main reason is that if you tell me too much, it could cloud the reading as we progress, causing interference along the channel established between the spirit and me. If I ask you a question and you answer it by telling me your husband's life story, it may make it difficult for me to figure out after that if something in my mind is from your husband or was put there by what you told me.

Of course, telling me as little as possible will also help you with validations as we go along. If I tell you I'm seeing a red convertible, and you tell me nothing more than the fact that it makes sense, and then I tell you something more specific about that convertible that few people or nobody could have known — such as the fact that it was the car he picked you up in for your first date forty years ago at a drive-in movie — then this becomes another validation for you; you didn't tell me anything that could have led me to say that.

People can also be skeptical of what I do because they have had bad experiences with other psychics or mediums and, as a result, lump us all into one group. It's similar to when people think all telemarketers are scam artists, or all politicians are crooked, or all car salesmen are manipulative. If they have had a bad experience with one or some, or have heard too many negative stories from other people about them, they may close their minds to all of them. It's not fair to anyone and could limit a skeptical person's opportunities, but I certainly understand why people might think that way.

Some who refuse to believe do so because they were taught by their religion that they aren't supposed to believe that I can do what I do. I count my own grandma among that group. Again, I entirely understand and respect that. I tried my hardest for years to not believe any of it myself, and it was happening right in my own head! Believe me, I get it! This is the dead we're dealing with. It's life beyond this one — one thing that few people know anything about and may not even want to know about.

If you leave one of my readings as a believer, it is my hope that you leave with the peace, healing, and hope that can positively transform your life, that in at least some small way I have helped strengthen your faith, given you a reason to keep pushing forward through difficult times, and provided comfort that may have previously eluded you.

When people walk away from one of my readings feeling better than before they came in, it generates an overwhelming feeling in me — a feeling of, more than anything else, gratitude to the spirits. In fact, as I stated earlier, I can sometimes feel the spirits thanking me with their energy — a tingling down my spine or chills throughout my body. Even if I can't feel it every time, I know they are grateful.

But I am the one who is most grateful — to them. I am grateful for this gift they have given me and for enabling me to make a significant impact in the world in such a positive way. That is why after each reading I find a quiet place, look up to the sky, raise my hands, and humbly say, "Thank you."

Thank you, God, and thank you, spirits, for gracing me with the unexpected and for trusting me to share this gift with those searching for what we all want in our lives every moment of every day: peace, healing, and hope.

ACKNOWLEDGMENTS

Thank you to every one of my friends and family members who have been with me throughout my journey — in life and with this book — for your unconditional support, guidance, and love. I would not be where I am today without you.

I especially want to thank:

My grandmother, for being so selfless and for raising me to be pure and honest with myself and others.

William Croyle, for sharing his gift and truly capturing my message for this book. I will always cherish your hard work, dedication, and empathy. Thank you for believing in me!

Georgia Hughes at New World Library, for the leadership and love you provided me through this process, from our very first phone chat to the final printed pages; and all the others at New World Library who contributed to the success of this project with their dedication and hard work, including Kristen Cashman, Tracy Cunningham, Tona Pearce Myers, Jonathan Wichmann, and Kim Corbin.

Ronald Goldfarb and Gerrie Sturman, for bringing me the perfect publisher; my assistant and dear friend, Zaul Hernandez, for all your hard work and dedication; and my partner, Patrick Markert, for helping me remain focused and centered each day.

To my dog, Teddy, who has been a faithful companion and taught me that love transcends words.

Jessica Jones, for believing in me and spreading the word to everyone you know.

Row Kinnear, Mary MacDonnell, Stephen M. Kappos, Susan J. Engel, Katie Nielsen, Lisa Schoenthal, Roxanne Resch, Shelly Krieger, Amy Brick, Esther Hickey, Diane Ciz, Lynn Fox, Lora Vestal Scott, Jennifer Horsman, Kristy Richey, Ursula Cloutier, and the few people who asked to remain anonymous, for your faith in my ability to bring you peace, healing, and hope and for openly sharing your experiences.

Christina Alba Rice, Kimberly Alba, Carolina Yasukawa, Lynnette Yasukawa, Michelle Larson, Iva Peele, Patricia Craig, Katy Sisco, Sylvia Anderson, Sindy Godfrey, Evelyn Erives, Tina Thomson, Judissa Atkinson, Jayne Rapp, Catherine Markert, Roxanne Vargas, Chris Fahey, and Tanya Brown, for your friendship and support.

Maureen Hancock, for your beautifully written foreword; Rebecca Rosen, for being such a guiding light; and Dorothy Lucey, Echo Bodine, Christine Woods, and Gary E. Schwartz, PhD, for your kind words and encouragement.

Carol Daria, Lisa Kovach, Melissa Marsh, Judy Jakyma, Debra Croyle, and Lee Ann Plunkett, for helping me craft my words in an understandable and impactful way.

Spirits and God, for guiding me toward my true calling.

And last but certainly not least — all my clients and fans. You have helped make me who I am today in a way that is difficult to repay. Thank you for believing in me.

ABOUT BILL PHILIPPS

Photo by Kate sZatmari

Bill Philipps is a psychic medium who helps the deceased communicate with their loved ones on earth. Bill's fresh, upbeat, and direct approach perfectly complements his warm and relatable demeanor, captivating audiences worldwide.

Bill studied opera at the San Francisco Conservatory of Music and graduated in 2008. He found that music, in a deeply spiritual way, enabled him to tune in to and further develop his psychic-medium abilities, which dated to his childhood. He gave readings while attending the conservatory and, after graduating, professionally pursued his true calling.

Bill has appeared on such television shows as *Dr. Phil*, and his clients include numerous celebrities. He conducts individual readings in person, by phone, or via Skype. He also offers small-group readings and large-audience readings throughout the United States. He lives in Southern California. You can learn more about Bill at www.billphilipps.com.

ABOUT WILLIAM CROYLE

Photo by Patrick Reddy

Coauthor William Croyle is a native of Cleveland, Ohio, and a graduate of St. Ignatius High School and Ashland University. He is the coauthor of *I Choose to Be Happy: A School Shooting Survivor's Triumph over Tragedy*, with Missy Jenkins Smith; *Angel in the Rubble: The Miraculous Rescue of 9/11's Last Survivor*, with Genelle Guzman-McMillan; and *Finding Peace Amid the Chaos: My Escape from Depression and Suicide*, with Tanya Brown. William lives in Erlanger, Kentucky, with his wife, Debra, and their three sons. More information on his books is available at www.williamcroyle.com.